PEWTER MARKS
OF THE WORLD

PEWTER MARKS OF THE WORLD

D. STARÁ

HAMLYN
London · New York · Sydney · Toronto

Translated by Joy Moss – Kohoutová
Marks drawings by Lenka Urbánková
Graphic design by Aleš Krejča
© Copyright Artia, Prague 1977
Reprinted 1978
Designed and produced by Artia
for The Hamlyn Publishing Group
Limited
London . New York . Sydney .
Toronto
Astronaut House, Feltham,
Middlesex, England
ISBN 0 600 37090 0
Printed in Czechoslovakia
by Polygrafia
2/10/03/51 – 2

CONTENTS

INTRODUCTION

Tin is a lustrous, silvery-grey, soft and malleable metallic element resistant to air, moisture and many acids. It is relatively indestructible, because tin utensils can be re-used as raw material, almost without loss, to make other pewterware.

Because of its advantageous properties, tin was a favourite working material from time immemorial. However, for technological reasons, especially because of its brittleness, tin was almost always used in combination with other elements; from ancient times, for instance, it was known that tin amalgamated with copper formed bronze. Therefore it should be pointed out that utensils sometimes said to be made of tin are actually products of alloys in which tin (the chemical element Stannum = Sn) predominates, but which contains other elements as well (lead, copper, bismuth, antimony, etc.). In most European languages there is no distinction between these two concepts of 'tin' as such and an alloy (German = Zinn, French = l'étain, Russian = olovo, Italian = peltro, Polish = cyna, Swedish = tenn, Czech = cín, etc.). In English, however, the chemical element is called tin while products made from a given alloy are known as pewter.

The production of pewterware was widespread in areas where tin deposits were found. Important European tin mines were worked in Cornwall, England, and in Central Europe the pewterers' craft began to develop after tin deposits were discovered in Bohemia and Saxony.

Although today this might seem somewhat exaggerated, pewter accompanied man from cradle to grave. The fashions of each period, sometimes more and sometimes less, influenced the shape and decoration of pewter items. Tableware and dishes to store food were made of pewter, as well as personal objects (pins, buttons, small boxes, etc.), children's toys and tin dishes and instruments used for medical purposes; from this lustrous malleable material guild flagons, ecclesiastical implements and small devotionals were made. Coffins and plates for coffins, the hands of tower clocks and even roof coverings were fashioned from pewter. But all these represent a limited area in which pewter appeared in everyday items because we have not mentioned the purely technical uses of pewter. Even so, it would be difficult today to itemize in detail the contribution made by pewter to different fields.

An important feature of pewter dishes was that their contact with food did not harm the human organism. But there was always the fear of poisoning from lead which, because it was more malleable, was used as the main alloy of pewter. The amount of lead was therefore restricted and carefully controlled to make certain that pewterers did not violate regulations stipulating the content of the alloy, especially since the price of lead was relatively much cheaper than that of tin.

From the time of the Middle Ages pewterware had pewter marks which, on the one hand, basically guaranteed the use of stipulated quality material and, on the other hand, were something in the nature of the craftsman's signature. From pewter marks one can often discover, even after many years, the name of the pewterer, the place where he lived, and in some instances the town where the guild to which he belonged was located. From these marks we also learn when the pewterer became a guild master and what alloys he used to make his products. Quite often the whole system of marks, or touches, helps us to determine the year in which the product was made. In the course of time the marks fell into three basic groups. Their shape, content and manner of use differed from one area of production to another and/or linked up to one another.

The town mark most often contained either a simplified version of the town's heraldic device or only a part of it, and sometimes another symbol of the locality. We also come across the name of the town written out. The date, as a rule, indicated when an important document was issued for the pewterers of that particular locality.

The master mark contained the initials or the full name of the master, his touch or an allegory of his name, or a religious motif he selected, an allegorical figure, etc. The date given on this touch usually denoted the year when the pewterer passed his examination and became a guild master. As a rule, this date was the same as the one when he was made a town burgher. The mark also tells us whether the ware dated from a period when the workshop was in the hands of the widow following the master's death.

The manner of marking in itself indicated the quality of the pewter used to make the utensils. In earlier times the use of town marks guaranteed the product's quality. Elsewhere, the number of stamped marks (for instance two for the town and one for the master, or one for the town and one for the master), signified the amount of lead in the alloy. Isolated *marks of quality* began to appear from the second half of the 16th century and towards the end of the 18th century these were very widespread. They revealed the provenance of the tin ore deposits and the amount of lead in the alloy.

In different countries and regions various symbols were used to indicate the quality of the pewter — but always with a view to the established local traditions, subject to the regulations in force. Both the Tudor rosette, originally characteristic of English pewter, and the figure of an angel, so popular from about 1700, became the universal symbol in later times for good quality. Tin without lead, or with a very small quantity of it, was indicated with the Latin letter X, the initials CL, F, etc. (When discussing the individual countries, emphasis is always placed on the most frequent manner of marking.)

In England, from the second half of the 18th century, and later in other countries too, an alloy containing, among other elements, antimony, was widely used. At first it was called a composition, but later it was generally known as Britannia metal. In some instances, however, it was already industrially processed with a press, in contrast to the basic pewtering technique of pouring the substance into a mould.

Look first in this book for the mark which is clearest on your pewter specimen. Look for it under the subject matter that forms the main content of the mark. If you are uncertain about the design in the mark, look for it under a similar one. It must be remembered that the marks were often very alike and differed only in minor details. These might escape you, since, in the course of time many marks became quite illegible. The marks sometimes depict simultaneously several subjects or concepts. Therefore look carefully under all motifs that are in the mark in order to decide which it is. When you have found the model of the mark in this book, then look in the same way for the other marks on your specimen. Compare them to see whether they are the same. The touch of master XYZ of town A must correspond to the mark of town A, etc. Read through the manner of stamping pewter in the given country where the town in which the pewterer worked is located. An outline of pewter marks with stress on the characteristic features of the individual countries can be found at the beginning of this publication.

If you are still uncertain about the mark, or have only found one that is similar to it, then study in greater detail the marks and manner of marking in the country which has the closest related touches. At the end of the chapters on the individual countries are bibliographies on this subject (or references to more detailed bibliographies), insofar as they exist.

The Christian name and surname of the masters, and also variants showing how they most frequently appeared in specialist literature, are to be found in the legends of the pewter touches. Next to every locality is the abbreviation of the state to which it belongs today. The present territorial adherence was observed because the borders of some states were very fluid throughout the centuries and in places changed hands several times. The names of the towns in the marks are given as they are used today, but the index at the end of the book includes their historical names or the names under which they are listed in specialist literature. A set of marks precedes each short chapter on the development and characteristic features of pewter touches in countries whose pewter signatures are included in this book. The selection of marks was guided by a desire to make orientation easier for the reader. Therefore this book is almost complete – in view of what is known on the subject – as regards the town mark, so important in determining the locality and country of origin of the specimens. The choice of master marks had to be limited in view of their vast number, but, even so, our selection represents the signatures of masters of different countries and historical periods, particularly of the 18th and 19th centuries. Earlier and later marks are mentioned only by way of example. The marks stamped on American pewterware produced from Britannia metal were usually factory marks and it would have been superfluous to have included them in this publication. But a list of their producers, with the presumed place in which and time when they worked, is included in: Laughlin, L. J.: *Pewter in America,* Vol. 2, p. 95 ff. Vol. 3, p. 174 ff. Barre, Vermont 1971. The catalogue starts from the assumption that the reader does not have a deep knowledge of the principles of pewter marking. The device in the mark was used as the guideline in arranging the order of this book and it is also the key to looking for the mark. This list makes no distinction as to whether the mark is one of a town, a master mark or a mark of quality. The entries to the marks give the Christian name or names and the surname of the pewterer or of the factory. Then the date when the pewterer passed the guild master's examination (M), and possibly when he was named a town burgher (B). Only in the event that this period could not be determined, we list for orientation purposes the year of the pewterer's birth (*) and wherever possible, the year of his death (†). In some instances we were able to indicate only the approximate period the pewterer worked: this is done by giving the year or dates that should be regarded merely as terms of reference, or sometimes simply the century.

The marks were arranged according to the following pattern: Letters in alphabetical order (1–377), Man and parts of his body, including allegorical figures etc. (378–639), Animals (640–934), Birds (935–1101), Plants (1102–1325), Architecture (1326–1432), Celestial bodies and symbols (1433–1483), Items (1484–1752), Touches (1753–1877), Combined touches (1878–1947), Oriental touches (1948–1960).

HISTORY OF MARKS
IN INDIVIDUAL STATES

AUSTRIA

A decree existed from the 16th century which makes clear that the local pewterers chiefly used two marks on their products, the master mark and the town mark, and later both were often combined into one mark. The two-mark system, employed until the 18th century in most parts of the country, designated an alloy of tin and lead in the proportion of 10 : 1. But conversely, the two-mark system was used, for instance, in the Salzburg area, and elsewhere, to indicate inferior quality alloys.

In the 18th century quality marks appeared. The Tudor rosette indicated products made from pewter known as *Feinzinn*. Whether the term *English Zinn* was stamped only on articles made of imported metal, or on tin purified in the English manner (*Purgiertes*), is not yet entirely clear. Marks showing an angel were also used to indicate that the pewter contained only a small quantity of lead.

Bibliography:

Hintze, E.: *Die deutschen Zinngiesser und ihre Marken.* Vol. 7. Leipzig 1931.
Mais, Ad.: *Die Zinngiesser Wiens.* In: *Jahrbuch des Vereins für Geschichte der Stadt Wien.* Vol. 14. Horn 1958. P. 7 ff.
Vetter, R. M. – Wacha, G.: *Linzer Zinngiesser.* Wien – München 1967.
Waidacher, F.: *Die Zinngiesser Familie Zamponi.* Graz 1967 (exhibition catalogue).
Wolfbauer, G.: *Die steirischen Zinngiesser und ihre Marken.* Graz 1934.

The oldest written record on using an alloy consisting of 10 parts of tin to 1 part of lead in the production of pewterware was issued by Prague pewter masters and dates from 1371. The Guild Statute of Brno Pewterers of 1378 already contains regulations on stamping pewter products and, simultaneously, notes the punishments to be meted out for failure to comply with this rule.

A mark of pewter quality was added during the 18th century to the town and master marks. It had been stamped on items sporadically from the 17th century, but only when a decree of Empress Maria Theresa was issued in 1770 did it become obligatory.

The use of the stipulated alloy of 10 parts of tin to 1 part of lead was additionally stressed quite often in the 18th century by the mark *Probezinn* (= P Z). Products made of Slavkov pewter were stamped *Schlaggenwalder Feinzinn* (= *SW Feinzinn*), whereas those made of tin from other Czech mines merely had the stamp *Feinzinn*. Beginning in 1770, utensils made from re-used pewter already combined with lead had to be stamped *Vermischtes Zinn*.

Bibliography:

Flodrová, M. – Samek, B.: *Cín ve sbírkách muzea města Brna*. Brno 1970.
Hintze, E.: *Die deutschen Zinngiesser und ihre Marken*. Vol. 4. Leipzig 1926.
Kapusta, J.: *Značkovaný cín olomoucké provenience ve sbírkách muzea v Olomouci*. In: *Sborník Vlastivědného muzea v Olomouci*, B VI/1960 (1962), pp. 133–169.
Stará D.: *Konvářské značky pražských mistrů*. Roztoky u Prahy 1974.
Tischer, F.: *Böhmisches Zinn*. Leipzig 1928 (New edition 1976).

CHINA

The oldest pewterware of Chinese origin is authenticated from the 18th century, but most pewter items are from the

19th and 20th centuries. They are either stamped with Chinese characters or Latin letters.

ENGLAND, IRELAND

The oldest ordinance of the Craft of Pewterers was drawn up in London, in 1348, and the first mention of pewter marks indicating the quality of the pewterware dates from 1474. In 1564 the Tudor rosette was used for the first time in a mark, and it later became a frequent symbol even in other countries for pewterware produced from the best quality metal.

The oldest marks contained the initials and heraldic device of the locality, and/or the coat of arms of the town (for instance Edinburgh) and the year the master 'opened shop'. The name of the town was sometimes the content of another, independent mark, just as were the quality marks. For items of exceptionally high grade 'Hard Metal' there existed from 1694 until the 18th century the symbol X, regarded in the 19th century as a universal guarantee of good pewter products.

In addition to the above-mentioned marks, from 1635 until the beginning of the 18th century smaller hallmarks in sets of four were used, similar to the tradition of goldsmiths' and silversmiths' hallmarks.

Bibliography:

Cotterell, H. H.: *Old Pewter. Its Makers and Marks.* (1st edition London 1929, 8th edition Tokyo 1974.)

FINLAND

In view of its historical relations, Finland was closely linked to pewtermaking in Sweden and in the other Baltic states.

Three types of alloys were used to produce pewterware, and the products were stamped accordingly. Those alloyed products containing

a) 97 parts of tin and 3 parts of lead had four marks – two of the town and two of the master;

b) 83 parts of tin and 17 parts of lead had three marks – one was the town mark and two were those of the master; and

c) 66 2/3 parts of tin to 33 1/3 of lead had one mark, that of the master.

Products made of English pewter, i. e. of an alloy without lead, had marks (the figure of an angel, a rosette, a device) which denoted the kind of metal used to produce the item.

In the master mark, the master stamped the initials of his own name and the first letter of the second part of a double name (see illustration).

According to the custom of stamping items made of precious metals, pewterers added to the town and master marks a mark showing the year the product was made. The latter had letters based on the following tables:

A	1694	A	1718	a (A)	1742	h (H)	1766	H 2	1790
B	1695	B	1719	b (B)	1743	i (I)	1767	I 2	1791
C	1696	C	1720	c (C)	1744	k (K)	1768	K 2	1792
D	1697	D	1721	d (D)	1745	l (L)	1769	L 2	1793
E	1698	E	1722	e (E)	1746	m (M)	1770	M 2	1794
F	1699	F	1723	f (F)	1747	n (N)	1771	N 2	1795
G	1700	G	1724	g (G)	1748	o (O)	1772	O 2	1796
H	1701	H	1725	h (H)	1749	p (P)	1773	P 2	1797
I	1702	I	1726	i (I)	1750	q (Q)	1774	Q 2	1798
K	1703	K	1727	k (K)	1751	r (R)	1775	R 2	1799
L	1704	L	1728	l (L)	1752	s (S)	1776	S 2	1800
M	1705	M	1729	m (M)	1753	t (T)	1777	T 2	1801
N	1706	N	1730	n (N)	1754	u (U)	1778	U 2	1802
O	1707	O	1731	o (O)	1755	w (W)	1779	W 2	1803
P	1708	P	1732	p (P)	1756	x (X)	1780	X 2	1804
Q	1709	Q	1733	q (Q)	1757	y (Y)	1781	Y 2	1805
R	1710	R	1734	r (R)	1758	z (Z)	1782	Z 2	1806
S	1711	S	1735	a (A)	1759	A 2	1783	A 3	1807
T	1712	T	1736	b (B)	1760	B 2	1784	B 3	1808
U	1713	U	1737	c (C)	1761	C 2	1785	C 3	1809
W	1714	W	1738	d (D)	1762	D 2	1786	I	1810
X	1715	X	1739	e (E)	1763	E 2	1787	II	1811
Y	1716	Y	1740	f (F)	1764	F 2	1788	III	1812
Z	1717	Z	1741	g (G)	1765	G 2	1789	IV	1813

Bibliography:

Gahlnbäck, J.: *Zinn und Zinngiesser in Finland*. Helsingfors 1925.
Löfgren, A.: *Finländska tenngjutare och deras stämpling före 1809*. Helsingfors 1927.

FRANCE

There is earlier evidence on the existence of pewter marks, but only with the 1643 decree of Louis XIII can we form a concrete picture of the situation. This decree stated that items made of fine tin (*L'étain fin*), also known as *Sonnant* (i.e. an alloy of tin containing less than ten per cent of lead), must have a mark with the name and symbol of the pewterer and stamped *étain fin*. For products made of alloys containing more lead, a mark with a crowned hammer or another special symbol and the pewterer's initials had to be used. At the bottom of the mark was the first letter of the name of the town where the pewter master worked (for instance P = Paris, B = Bordeaux, C = Chartres, E = Etampes, M = = Melun, R = Rouen).

Edicts were issued in 1657 and 1674 on collecting state taxes for pewter control. In 1691 a scale of fees was established and the state control mark had to be stamped on pewter products, just as it had to be on items made of precious metals. This mark contained the date, the name of the town or its first letter, the pewterer's initials, and additionally the kind of tin, or only the first letter (for instance F = *étain fin*, C = *étain commun*). From 1728 the letters CE were added (*claire étoffe*) calling attention to the fact that the alloy contained a considerable amount of lead, which meant that pewterware made from it should not be used either to serve or to store food.

Bibliography:

Guilbert-Guieu, M.—Breton, Y.: *Les étains. Trésors des Musées d'Angers*. Angers 1973.
Tardy: *Les étains français*. Paris 1956.
Tardy: *Les poinçons des étains français*. Paris 1974.

The earliest mention of marks to be stamped on pewterware dates from the 14th and 15th centuries (Hamburg 1375, 1461). The first report from Nuremberg, the best known German pewter centre, is dated 1578 although, evidently, pewterware was stamped prior to this date. The Nuremberg test (*Probe*), often also called *zum Zehnten*, denoted an alloy of ten parts of tin to one part of lead. Many later pewterers referred to it as *gemeine Reichsprobe*. However, it was not the only alloy used on German territory. There was, for instance, the *Kölner Probe* (6:1), valid in Cologne on the Rhine, in the Main and Hanover areas; a number of other types of alloys were also used in the different regions according to local customs. A mark of quality was later added to those of the town and the master. In some places these were combined into a single mark (for instance, Augsburg, Nuremberg). An alloy with ten parts of tin to one part of lead was used in Thuringia and in some Saxonian towns and was shown by the Latin letter X. Pure tin, tin purified the English way, and *Feinzinn* had a mark with a rosette, most often with a crown, or with the figure of an angel. Good quality alloy, for instance, was also denoted, apart from the usual marks, by a *Land mark* (Württemberg and Baden). In other regions, instead of the mark of quality there was a special manner of marking – the town or the master's mark was stamped three times. This so-called three-mark system was used from 1614 in Saxony. It was also used in Upper Lusatia, Lübeck, Rostock and Württemberg.

The numbers 13, 74, 08 and 1708, which often appeared in the three-mark system, indicate the Saxonian origin of the products. In Saxony a decree was issued in 1614 and reaffirmed in 1674 and 1708, stipulating the proportion of metals a tin alloy had to contain.

Conversely, the numbers 79 and 33 indicate that the product comes from Lübeck, where similar decrees were issued in 1579 and 1633, in Bayreuth in 1689, in Regensburg in 1692, and Backnang in 1749.

Bibliography:
Bauer, D.: *Kirchliches Zinngerät aus dem Kreise Marburg.* Marburg 1970.

Haedeke, H.-U.: *Zinn*. 2nd edition Braunschweig 1973.
Haedeke, H.-U.: *Sächsisches Zinn*. Leipzig 1975.
Hintze, E.: *Die deutschen Zinngiesser und ihre Marken*.
  Vol. 1—7. Leipzig 1921–1931.
Kohlmann, Th.: *Zinngiesserhandwerk und Zinngerät in Olden-burg, Ostfriesland und Osnabrück (1600-1900)*. Göttingen 1972.
Mory, L.: *Schönes Zinn*. 4th edition München 1972.
Pieper-Lippe, M.: *Zinn im Südlichen Westfalen*. Münster 1974.
Reinheckel, G.: *Nürnberger Zinn*. Dresden 1971.
Wittichen, M.: *Celler Zinngiesser*. Celle 1967.

HUNGARY

During the 16th century pewterers' guilds were set up on the territory of Hungary. The use of pewter marks stamped on items is authenticated from this century.

During the 18th century a touch of quality was added to the marks of the town and the master. From 1770, when Empress Maria Theresa issued a decree restricting the amount of lead that could be used in production, it was obligatory to have this touch on all products.

The alloy of ten parts of tin to one part of lead (*Probzinn* = *PZ*) was the one most frequently used for pewterware. In some areas this *PZ* touch was employed to indicate an alloy in a ratio of 9 : 1, but which was not permitted to have more than 10 per cent lead. Inferior quality items were stamped *Probe zum Vierten* (4 : 1). *Feinzinn* either contained no lead at all, or only a very small amount of it which in no circumstances could exceed 10 : 1; it also was shown by a rosette under a crown or the abbreviation *FZ*. Work with English tin was marked *Englisch Zinn* or *Rein*, and/or *Fein Englisch Zinn*, and had the mark of an angel.

Pewterers on the territory of today's Hungary worked chiefly in Budapest, Györ, Sopron, Debrecen and Miskolc.

Bibliography:

Hintze, E.: *Die deutschen Zinngiesser und ihre Marken*. Vol. 7.
  Leipzig 1931.
Weiner, P.: *Old Pewter in Hungarian Collections*. Budapest
  1971.

ITALY

Very few pewter items have survived and only some have pewter marks. Most of the marks seem to come from the southern Tirol and Venice. No other information about the pewter marks used is known because the area has not yet been thoroughly studied.

JAPAN

The production of pewterware in Japan is of relatively recent date. From 1890 markings to indicate pewter quality were introduced and they denoted 80, 95 and 99 per cent tin alloys.

The items also have the stamps of the producer, written either with Japanese characters or Latin letters. But there is an authenticated instance in which the mark of an outstanding producer denoted items made of 80 per cent tin alloys.

NETHERLANDS

The oldest decrees making pewter touches obligatory date from the Middle Ages, and the first pewter marks are from the town of Groningen in the second half of the 15th century. From the 16th century individual pewter items usually had the touch of the master craftsman and of the town. The quality of the pewter was not subject to a uniform standard, but a town mark on an item was generally proof of its good quality. From the 15th century a touch with a crowned hammer, sometimes also with the initials of the master, and later with a rosette, began to be used to indicate good quality.

The rosette under a crown and initials was the most frequently used touch, combining the master's mark and the mark of quality pewter. In the 18th century, small rectangular touches, similar to those used to stamp silver and probably an imitation of English hallmarks, began to be used.

Bibliography:

Dubbe, B.: *Tin en tinngieters in Nederland.* Zeist 1965.

POLAND

The existence of pewterers from the 14th century is corroborated in archive material. The earliest reports on obligatory use of pewter marks (Elbląg, Malbork) date from the first half of the 15th century. The proportion of tin to lead in the alloy used by pewterers often differed in the individual cities and/or territorial areas, and in addition, stipulations regarding the quality of the pewter changed in the course of time. This also affected the manner of marking pewterware.

Except for the earliest, individually authenticated items, most stamped pewter products are from the 18th century. In addition to touches of the master craftsman and the town, according to the regulations valid in the particular locality there also was a touch depicting St John, an eagle or rosette denoting the use of top quality pewter alloy. (For example, Toruń 1523 – St John, 1612 – an eagle, 1749 – a rosette; Kołobrzeg and other towns – a rosette, etc.) The touch with the figure of an angel usually indicates that English tin was used. The names *Kronnzinn* and *Feinzinn* were employed in the 18th century for an alloy of tin and lead prepared in a proportion of 15 parts of tin to one part of lead, and had three marks topped by a crown. In Gdańsk the term *Sonant* was used to indicate the quality of the pewter. In some localities the words *Alte Probe* had to be stamped on products recast from old alloys containing lead whose use was forbidden from 1735 in towns in the production of pewter items (Słupsk, Szczecin).

Bibliography:

Hintze, E.: *Die deutschen Zinngiesser und ihre Marken.* Vol. 3. *Norddeutschen Zinngiesser.* Vol. 4. Leipzig 1923; *Schlesische Zinngiesser.* Leipzig 1926.

Michalska, J.: *Cyna w dawnych wiekach*. Kraków 1973 (containing a bibliography).
Myslińska, J.: *Konwisarstvo toruńskie XVII – XVIII. w.* Warsaw 1968.

ROMANIA

The earliest substantiated reports about obligatory pewter marks on pewterware are to be found in articles of the Transylvanian guilds dating from the 16th century.

In the 18th century a quality mark was added to the original town and master marks on pewter items.

Pewterers were active chiefly in Braşov, Cluj, Sibiu and Sighişoara.

Bibliography:

Haldner, A.: *Colectia de cositoare*. Sibiu 1972.
Hintze, E.: *Die deutschen Zinngiesser und ihre Marken*. Vol. 7. Leipzig 1931, p. 415 ff.
Huber, H. — Oertel, G.: *Siebenbürgisch-sächsisches und anderes Zinn*. Reichenberg 1936.

RUSSIA

From the time of a decree issued by Peter the Great in 1722 pewter items had to be stamped. Until then they were marked only sporadically with pewterers' touches. This decree applied at first only to Moscow and St Petersburg (Leningrad). Unstamped items produced at this time, or even later, were evidently made in monastery workshops or in non-residential towns. The master mark was usually without symbols – only words or letters written on two lines in Cyrillic script. It contained the surname and Christian name of the master (Мастер), and ЦМ the guild master (Цеховой мастер).

Pewterware produced in pewter workshops in the Baltic

region is distinguished by the fact that the manner of marking started from the quality of the pewter used. Products made of an alloy with a small content of lead, which in this region was known as master's pewter, had three pewter touches, i.e. one of the town, and two of the master. Pewterware with a larger proportion of lead had only two touches: the town and the master's. Products made of English pewter, or of pewter purified in the English manner, were given two touches: a rosette and the master's mark. Stamping items with four small right-angled touches was evidently analogous to English silver hallmarks.

We also find other signatures of Russian-made products. Most often these were the marks of the engravers who decorated the pewter items and liked to engrave their initials on the underside of elaborately decorated plates. The marks of the owners are sometimes erroneously thought to be pewter touches; the most frequent of these are the symbols of the Tsar's and the patriarchal courts.

Bibliography:

Gahlnbäck, J.: *Russisches Zinn*. Leipzig 1928.
Gahlnbäck, J.: *Zinn und Zinngiesser in Liv-, Est- und Kurland*. Leipzig 1929.
Hintze, E.: *Die deutschen Zinngiesser und ihre Marken*. Vol. 4. Leipzig 1926.

SWEDEN

According to the earliest Swedish regulations of 1545, pewter utensils had to have pewter touches. The decree of 1694 indicated more precisely the exact manner of stamping the ware so that it corresponded to the quality of the alloys used.

Products of alloys containing

a) 97 per cent tin were given four touches: two were the master's and two the town's,

b) 83 per cent tin had three touches: two were the master's and one the town's,

c) 66 2/3 per cent of tin had two master's touches.

Starting from 1694 a mark with a rosette under a crown indicated utensils produced in the English manner from alloys containing no lead. In the master's marks were his initials and the first letter of the first syllable of the second part of a double-name.

From 1754 the government took charge of pewterware production and all high quality items were additionally stamped with a small touch that had three crowns, as the official guarantee of good quality.

From 1694 onwards date letters were engraved by pewterers on their items and these define precisely when each was made.

The following table indicates to which year the individual letters belong:

	I	II	III		IV (I)
A	1694	1718	1742	A	1759
B	1695	1719	1743	B	1760
C	1696	1720	1744	C	1761
D	1697	1721	1745	D	1762
E	1698	1722	1746	E	1763
F	1699	1723	1747	F	1764
G	1700	1724	1748	G	1765
H	1701	1725	1749	H	1766
I	1702	1726	1750	I	1767
K	1703	1727	1751	K	1768
L	1704	1728	1752	L	1769
M	1705	1729	1753	M	1770
N	1706	1730	. 1754	N	1771
O	1707	1731	. 1755	O	1772
P	1708	1732	. 1756	P	1773
Q	1709	1733	. 1757	Q	1774
R	1710	1734	. 1758	R	1775
S	1711	1735		S	1776
T	1712	1736		T	1777
V	1713	1737		V	1778
W	1714	1738		W	1779
X	1715	1739		X	1780
Y	1716	1740		Y	1781
Z	1717	1741		Z	1782

	2	3	4	5	6	7
A	1783	1807	1831	1855	1879	1903
B	1784	1808	1832	1856	1880	1904
C	1785	1809	1833	1857	1881	1905
D	1786	1810	1834	1858	1882	1906
E	1787	1811	1835	1859	1883	1907
F	1788	1812	1836	1860	1884	1908
G	1789	1813	1837	1861	1885	1909
H	1790	1814	1838	1862	1886	1910
I	1791	1815	1839	1863	1887	1911
K	1792	1816	1840	1864	1888	1912
L	1793	1817	1841	1865	1889	
M	1794	1818	1842	1866	1890	
N	1795	1819	1843	1867	1891	
O	1796	1820	1844	1868	1892	
P	1797	1821	1845	1869	1893	
Q	1798	1822	1846	1870	1894	
R	1799	1823	1847	1871	1895	
S	1800	1824	1848	1872	1896	
T	1801	1825	1849	1873	1897	
U	1802	1826	1850	1874	1898	
V	1803	1827	1851	1875	1899	
X	1804	1828	1852	1876	1900	
Y	1805	1829	1853	1877	1901	
Z	1806	1830	1854	1878	1902	

Bibliography:

Bruzelli, B.: *Tenngjutare i Sverige*. Stockholm 1967 (including a bibliography).
Löfgren, A.: *Det Svenska Tenngjutarehantverkets Historia*. Vol. 1–3. Stockholm 1925–1950.

SWITZERLAND

The earliest pewter marks date from the 16th century. In general three basic types of touches were used (the master's, the town's, and a mark of quality), but the manner in which they were applied varied in the individual cantons and towns.

differing from one another according to local regulations; the kind of pewter used was also different. The earliest type was the so-called *Zürcher Probe*, an alloy with four parts of tin to one part of lead. From the end of the 17th century an alloy containing a smaller amount of lead was used more frequently. If a maximum of 10 percent of lead was used, the item was marked with the letter F under a crown, or in French Switzerland with the words *Estain*, *Estin*, *Etain fin*, *fin cristallin*. There are also marks with the words *Blockzinn*, *Feinzinn*, *Englischzinn*, denoting the quality of the pewter. Utensils with the figure of an angel appeared after 1700; these were stamped on an item three times, next to each other.

An alloy of tin and lead that was customarily used and officially recognized could not contain more than 17 parts of lead to 100 parts of tin. In the French area it was marked with the words *étain commun* or with the letter C (= *commun*) and the date recalling the year the decree was issued establishing the proportion of tin to lead in the alloy.

Bibliography:

Bossard, G.: *Die Zinngiesser der Schweiz und ihr Werk*. Vol. 1. Zug 1920; Vol. 2. Zug 1934.
Schneider, H.: *Zinn*. Vol. 3. *Die Zinngiesser der Schweiz und ihre Marken. Olten und Freiburg im B.* (In preparation)

UNITED STATES OF AMERICA

The first pewterers, who arrived with English settlers, began producing pewterware during the 17th century. However, the earliest surviving pewter products date from the beginning of the 18th century. Production at the beginning was strongly influenced by imported English utensils. In contrast to European countries, there were no regulations in the States on the stamping of pewter products. Local pewter marks were more often those of a firm, and were considered a protective mark indicating the quality of the pewter.

Producers stamped larger marks chiefly on platters, dishes

and other flat items which carried the name of the pewterer and/or the town where he worked. The name of the town was sometimes given in a special, separate touch. Smaller touches with the producers' initials were stamped on the handle, thumbpieces, lugs, and so on. Until 1755, frequent subjects of the touches were the Tudor rosette with a crown, lion and unicorn; later that of an eagle was more commonplace. In addition, there was sometimes a quality mark in the form of the letter X (a crowned Roman ten).

Apart from the above-mentioned types of touches, between about 1750 and 1800 there appeared small hallmarks, deliberate imitations of silver hallmarks, that were stamped two to four times on pewter items.

Bibliography:

Laughlin, L. J.: *Pewter in America*. Vol. 1–3. Barre, Vermont 1971.

Marks of quality: a) *Probe zum Zehnten*, b) *clar und lauter*, c) *Probzinn*, d) *Schlaggenwalder Feinzinn*, e) *Feinzinn*, f) *Alte Probe*, g) *Sonant*

Mark with the master's initials and the first letter of the second part of his divided name (Petter Petterson, Helsinki – SF, 3rd quarter of 18th century).

Mark of the pewterer's widow (Christoph Lipmann, Elbląg — PL, M 1771 + 1778).

Marks imitating the silversmiths' marks (Johann Hayen III, Riga — SU, M 1772 + 1821).

PLATES

A — Austria
CH — Switzerland
CS — Czechoslovakia
D — Federal Republic
of Germany
DDR — German Democratic
Republic
DK — Denmark
F — France
GB — Great Britain
I — Italy
IRL — Ireland
J — Japan
NL — Netherlands
PL — Poland
R — Romania
RC — China
S — Sweden
SF — Finland
SU — Soviet Union
USA — United States
of America
YU — Yugoslavia

ABBREVIATIONS:

* date of birth
† date of death
B date acquired status of Burgh-
er of a given town
M date acquired status of guild
Master
Other dates indicate approxi-
mate time the pewterer worked.

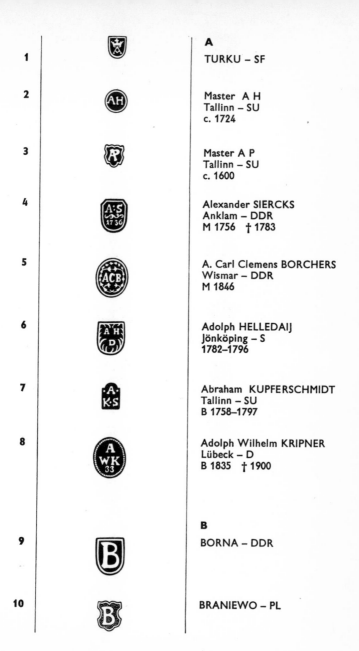

1

A

TURKU – SF

2

Master A H
Tallinn – SU
c. 1724

3

Master A P
Tallinn – SU
c. 1600

4

Alexander SIERCKS
Anklam – DDR
M 1756 † 1783

5

A. Carl Clemens BORCHERS
Wismar – DDR
M 1846

6

Adolph HELLEDAIJ
Jönköping – S
1782–1796

7

Abraham KUPFERSCHMIDT
Tallinn – SU
B 1758–1797

8

Adolph Wilhelm KRIPNER
Lübeck – D
B 1835 † 1900

9

B

BORNA – DDR

10

BRANIEWO – PL

11		Joseph BRANDEL Bolesławiec – PL 1813/14 – † 1876
12		Benjamin FALCK Pärnu – SU 1783 † 1808
13		Master B T Tartu – SU 1775

C

14		KRISTIANSTAD – S
15		Claude ADAM Chalon-sur-Saône – F 1708
16		Carl BEHMANN I Detern – D * 1831 † 1894 Oldenburg
17		BORDEAUX – F c. 1700 (*étain commun*)
18		CHEVILLARD Paris – F 1830–1850
19		Christian HOLSTEIN Neubrandenburg – DDR M 1713 † 1764
20		Cyriakus KLINTH Riga – SU 1540 † 1592

21		Conrad PRESS Anklam – DDR M 1735
22		Johann Caspar SCHMITZ Löningen – D M 1817 † 1837
23	C.D.F.	Carl de FLON Vaxjö – S 1777–1817
24		Carl Friedrich BURMEISTER Jr. Schwerin – DDR M 1798 † 1835
25		Carl Friedrich COFFRIED Liepaja – SU 1796 † 1836
26		Carl Heinrich Ferdinand FARNOW Neubrandenburg – DDR M 1836
27		Carl Hinrich KRAETZ Kiel – D M 1784 † 1828
28		Christoph Moritz KRAETZ Kiel – D M 1734 † after 1787
29		C. T. FRITSCH Greifswald – DDR M 1835
30		Christian Volrath HAUSHERR Stralsund – DDR M 1812

31		Carl Wilhelm JUCHANOWITZ Gdańsk – PL M 1811
32		Carl Christoph Friedrich OESTERLING Heide – D * 1827 † 1857
33		Christian Hermann HÜLSEMANN Lübeck – D M 1791 † 1832
34		ABBEVILLE – F beginning of 18th cent.

D

35		Diedrich HACKER Tallinn – SU M 1722 † 1770
36		Detloff Andreas Christian HAUSHERR Güstrow – DDR M 1805–1850 (mark used from 1814)
37		Daniel Friedrich BORCHWARDT Güstrow – DDR M 1743 † after 1767
38		Daniel Henrik LINDEGREA Lovisa – SF after middle of 18th cent.
39		Master D R K Sighişoara – R 17th cent.

E

40		ELBLĄG – PL

41		ELBLĄG – PL
42		CHEB – CS
43		ESSLINGEN – D

F

44		François AMELINE Chalon-sur-Saône – F 1710
45		Frederick BASSETT New York – USA 1761–1780
46		Friedrich MATTHIESSEN Hamburg – D M 1802 † 1822
47		Carl REUTLINGER Frankfurt a. M. – D M 1768 † 1809
48		Johann Abraham KLINGLING Frankfurt a. M. – D M 1669
49		Friedrich Arnold HÖLSCHER Fürstenau – D * 1758 – last quarter of 18th cent.

G

50		GRYFÓW ŚLĄSKI – PL

51		ST. GALLEN – CH
52		GÄWLE – S
53		Master G Jihlava – CS turn of 16th – 17th cent.
54		GÄWLE – S
55		GLOGÓW – PL
56		Heinrich GERHOLD Nysa – PL M 1782 † 1808
57		HRADEC KRÁLOVÉ – CS
58		C. GOTTESPFENNIG Rostock – DDR M 1832 † 1862
59		Master G B Sighişoara – R 17th cent.?
60		GÖTEBORG – S

61		Gerhard Heinrich ECKHOLT Haselünne – D * 1776 † 1830
62		Gilbert LEYDING Flensburg – D M 1756 † 1792
63		Master G K Sighişoara – R 17th cent.
64		Gideon RIDDER Riga – SU M 1591(?) † 1626
65		Gustav SILOV Linköping – S 1846–47 Vimmerby – S 1848–1875
66		George STIER Tallinn – SU M 1763 † 1781
67		Master G J H Tallinn – SU 1766
68		Gottfried Jacob SCHRÖDER Celle – D B 1829 † 1880
69		Gottlob Friedrich BAUMANN Hudiksvall – S 1789–1826
70		Georg Wilhelm HEDECKEN Eckernförde – D M 1736

71 Georg Christian Gottfried
DRÜHL
Hamburg – D
M 1812 † 1829

72 Gerhard Anton v. GLAN
Leer – D
M 1855 † 1890

H

73 Johann Gottfried
HASELBACH
Lwówek Śląski – PL
M 1800 –1831

74 HEDEMORA – S

75 Heinrich ECKHOLT
Meppen – D
* 1806 – second quarter of
19th cent.

76 Heinrich Johann Friedrich
HEYDEN
Grabow – DDR
1832 † 1858

77 Johan Jacob Heinrich
KRUMBÜGEL
Röbel – DDR
M 1806 † 1854

78 Master H R
Riga – SU
c. 1650

79 Henrik Philip STICKLER
Hälsingborg – S
1813—1851

80 Hans Bernhardt PFISTER
Graz – A
M 1703–1749

81	Hans Christoph REINCKE Rostock – DDR M 1799 † 1839
82	Henrich Gottlieb FLEMMING Johanngeorgenstadt – DDR M 1799
83	Joseph Heinrich BRINKMANN Friesoythe – D * 1811 – second third of 19th cent.
84	Hinrich PÖÖMÖLLER Liepaja – SU 1652–1699
85	Hans Wilhem MERCKEL Jihlava – CS second half of 17th cent.
86	Hinrich Wilhelm CONRADY Schleswig – D M 1786 † after 1800 (mark used from 1792)
87	Hermann Christoph HÜLSEMANN Lübeck – D M 1824 † 1864
88	Hans Christian Thomas GROTH Heide – D M 1768 † before 1813
89	Joseph Heinrich SETZER Heilbronn – D * 1768 † 1802
90	**I J** CHERNYAKHOVSK – SU

91	Johann Jochim BASS Waren – DDR M 1793 (Rostock) † 1832
92	Johan HAYEN I Riga – SU 1707 † 1752
93	Joseph LEDDELL New York – USA 1712–1753
94	Jochim SCHUH Tallinn – SU B 1613
95	Johann Georg SCHRÖDER Neuruppin – DDR M 1807
96	Jochim Andreas Wilhelm WESTPHAL Preetz – D M 1813 † 1843
97	Johann Balthasar ECKELMANN Bramsche – D third quarter of 18th cent.
98	John Carruthers CRANE Bewdley – GB 1800–1838
99	Joachim Christian DRÜHL Plau – DDR M 1715 † 1767
100	Johann Christopher HEYNE Lancaster – USA 1754–1780

101		Joachim Christopher HEITMANN Preetz – D M 1792 † 1838
102		Johann Christian PRESS Gnoien – DDR * 1779 † 1840
103		Jacob Christian WELLING Tartu – SU B 1755 † 1773
104		Johan Frederik WERRENRATH Lund – S 1847–1900
105		Johann Friedrich WAGNER Esslingen – D M 1749 † before 1816
106		Johann Gustav ALMQUIST Turku – SF first quarter od 19th cent.
107		Johann Gottfried FRITSCH Greifswald – DDR M 1800
108		Johann Gottfried HÜTTING Lübeck – D M 1802 † 1842
109		Johann George STIER Tallinn – SU B 1720 † 1767
110		Johann Georg TEUFEL Munich – D M 1756 † 1782

111		Johann Georg WINCKLER Lindau – DDR 1824 † 1874
112		Johann Heinrich OLDING Sögel – D c. 1862
113		Johann Heinrich Friedrich SCHLICHTING Bützow – DDR M 1850
114		Johann Jochim ALSTORFF Güstrow – DDR M 1724 † before 1741
115		Johann Jacob BASEDOW Lüneburg – D M 1822 † after 1850
116		Johann Joseph HARSCH Graz – A M 1693–1755
117		Johann Jürgen Christian KRIPNER Mölln – D M 1799 † 1829
118		Johann Joachim ULRICH Rendsburg – D M 1776 – beginning of 19th cent.
119		Johan Petter FAGERSTRÖM Kalmar – S 1798–1837
120		Jonas SJÖBERG Varberg – S 1743–1763

K

121		KARLSTADT – D
122		Johann Gottfried KIESEL Leisnig – DDR M 1815
123		Johann Ludwig Wilhelm KAWE Perleberg – DDR M 1770 † 1806

L

124		LICHTENSTEIG – CH
125		LANGRES – F
126		Lars BERG Karlstad – S 1743–1766
127		L. DRESCO Paris – F 1880–1904
128		Ludwig POPPE Essen – D * 1807 † 1852
129		LOVISA – SF
130		Lars Claesson FRIES Strängnäs – S 1760–1790

131		Master L T Tallinn – SU 1600
132		Louis PELLETIER Paris – F 1720
133		**M** Johann Friedrich MIX Nysa – PL M 1807
134		KOZUCHÓW – PL
135		MILTENBERG – D
136		VÄSTERÅS – S
137		Magnus BERGMAN Malmö – S 1794–1809
138		CHAVENTRÉ Paris – F 1835–1865
139		Matthias Nielson FLOWEEN Narva – SU 1732 † 1741
140		Matthias HÖLSCHER Quakenbrück – D * 1719 † 1793

141		Master M K Sighişoara – R 17th cent.
142		Martin Gustaf MOBERG Jönköping – S 1777–1815

N

143		UUSIKAUPUNKI – SF
144		Nicolaus JUSTELIUS Eksjö – S 1784–1819
145		Niclas Adolph FALCK Skara – S 1787–1828
146		Nicolas LAKE Vänersborg – S 1751–1781
147		Nicolas BOICERVOISE Paris – F 1771

P

148		PARCHIM – DDR
149		Petter HÖIJER Örebro – S 1796–1819
150		Peter KIRBY New York – USA 1736–1788

151	P. MORANE Paris – F 1875
152	Petter Samuelsson NORÉN Hedemora – S 1760–1797
153	Paul WEISE Zittau – DDR second half of 16th cent. † 1591
154	Peter JOUNG New York and Albany – USA 1775–1795
155	Peter Joseph BOROCCO Sen. Lörrach – D 1776–1806
156	Peter G. RAHNCKE Rostock – DDR M 1846 † after 1865
157	Peter Larsson HOLMIN Borås – S 1777–1793
158	Petter ÖHLERG Kristianstad – S 1780–1812
159	Pehr Henrik LUNDÉN Linköping – S 1797–1834
160	**R** RESZEL – PL

161		RORSCHACH – CH
162		RAUMA – SF
163		ROSTOCK – DDR
164		**S** STRZELIN – PL
165		STRZELIN – PL
166		SCHWEINFURT – D
167		ZAGAŃ – PL
168		Sven EKSTRÖM Norrköping – S 1824–1852
169		SZPROTAWA – PL
170		Simon SANDERS Langtree, nr. Bideford – GB c. 1700

171		Sven BERGLUND Malmö – S 1811–1844
172		Samuel WEIGANG Stockholm – S 1778–1793
		T
173		Timothy BRIGDEN Albany – USA 1816–1819
174		Master T K Sighişoara – R 17th cent.
		U
175		UDDEVALLA – S
		W
176		Jacob WOLFF Tartu – SU B 1751 † 1754
177		WROCŁAW – PL
178		VISBY – S
179		WROCŁAW – PL
180		WÄXJÖ – S

181		VYBORG – SU
182		VÄNERSBORG – S
183		VARBERG – S
184		VIMMERBY – S
185		Friedrich Wilhem NICOLAI Neubrandenburg – DDR B 1782 † 1846
186		Wilhem HELLEDAY Stockholm – S 1782–1830

Z

187		ZITTAU – DDR
188		ZÜRICH – CH
189		Zacharias LINDSTRÖM Tallinn – SU B 1804–1843
190		Andreas Ludwig ECKELMANN Lauenburg a. Elbe – D M 1768 † 1804

CALLIGRAPHIC LETTERS

191   Andreas DAHLIN
Ystad – S
1772–1799

192   Jochim Christoph David
BERTZOW
Neubrandenburg – DDR
B 1782   † 1829

193   Bernhard Johann
FAHRENKRÜGER
Hamburg – D
M 1798   † 1732(?)

194   Christian Jacob
BECKENDORFF
Glückstadt – D
B 1765   † 1815

195   Christian Joachim Friedrich
BOTEFÜHR
Neustadt / Glewe – DDR
M 1787   † 1831

196   Jochim Daniel
GOTTESPFENNIG
Rostock – DDR
M 1788

197   Johann Jacob GESNER
Kiel – D
M 1775   † 1818

198   Jacob Hinrich MEYER
Hamburg / Altona – D
B 1771

199   Johann Hinrich DAHM
Hamburg – D
M 1794   † probably 1824

200   Joachim Christian HENSKY
Plau – DDR
* 1766–1791

201		Carl Gottfried KLEMM Jr. Reichenbach (Vogtl.) – DDR M 1797 † 1835
202		Johann Carl Gottlob REICHEL Marienberg – DDR first half of 19 cent.
203		Lorentz SCHULTZ Liepaja – SU M 1711–1755
204		Master C B S Tallinn – SU c. 1765
205		Peter Georg SCHWINGER Kiel – DDR M 1721 † 1744
206		Gottlieb Wilhelm August MEYER Celle – D M 1762 † 1786
207		Johann WEIß Tallinn – SU B 1682 † 1727
208		Christian GRELL Demmin – DDR M 1725 † 1745
209		Johann Sebastian STIER Tallinn – SU M 1744 † 1779
210		Johann George STIER Tallinn – SU B 1720 † 1767

211		George STIER Tallinn – SU M 1763 † 1781
212		Joachim Christian HENSKY Röbel – DDR M 1763 † 1822
213		Johann Friedrich Christian DRÜHL Sternberg – DDR M 1762 † 1788
214		Johann Gottlieb DRÜHL Bützow – DDR second half of 18th cent.
215		Christian Heinrich SCHLÖR Sen. Kunzelsau – D M 1793 (?) † 1837

OWNERS MARKS

216		Schwen BRAHT Rehna – DDR M 1714 † 1749
217		Johann Friedrich RECKEN Pritzwalk – DDR M 1757
218		Johann Friedrich SCHRÖDER Horneburg bei Stade – D M 1767
219		Hermann Anton Diedrich SPIESKE I Oldenburg – D M 1767 † 1809
220		Heinrich Ludolf KÖSTER Hamburg / Altona – D * 1708 (?) † 1763

221		Nicolaus Gerhard **HANSMANN** Oldenburg – D M 1763 † 1808
222		Jochim **SCHULTE III** Wismar – DDR M 1694 † 1736
223		Johan Heinrich **SCHÜNEMANN** Celle – D M 1698 † 1711
224		Daniel Martin **ALSTORFF** Güstrow – DDR M 1699
225		Johann **PALHEYDT** Mölln – D M 1663
226		Nicolaus **RÖHRDANTZ** Rostock – DDR M 1717 † after 1748
227		Jacob **TIMMERMANN** Glückstadt – D M 1722 † 1759
228		Johann Matthias **TIMMERMANN** Jr. Hamburg – D M 1751 † after 1776
229		Matthias **CLASSEN** Hamburg – D M 1667/68 † 1710
230		Benjamin **PEWES** Gdańsk – PL M 1701

231		Claus HANSMANN Oldenburg – D M 1724 † 1758
232		Hinrich BRUMMER Jr. Hamburg – D M 1721
233		Erich WITTER Grabow – DDR M 1698 † 1721
234		Johann MÄGEBEHR Lübeck – D last quarter of 17th cent. † 1710
235		Jochim Hinrich SCHRÖDER Stralsund – DDR B 1720
236		Bartholomaeus KLOTT Greifswald – DDR M 1702
237		Peter REESE Tallinn – SU B 1708 † 1754
238		Jochim SENSS Tallinn – SU 1680–1710
239		Master P R I Tallinn – SU c. 1695
240		Master C G Riga – SU c. 1694

241		Jacob (?) BRASCHKE Gdańsk – PL M 1700
242		Daniel NEUMANN Stade – D M 1680
243		Master T G Prešov – CS c. 1661
244		Heinrich Samuel SCHILLER Szprotawa – PL active in second half of 18th cent.
245		Andreas WÖSTHOFF Rostock – DDR M 1673 † 1726
246		Pavel KOPES Tallinn – SU B 1670 † 1694
247		Peter MEESE Riga – SU B 1569 † 1683 (?)
248		Claus SCHMIDT Riga – SU B 1690–1710
249		Hans KÖHLER Hamburg – D M 1661 † 1695
250		Jürgen MEYER III Celle – D B 1667 † 1704

251		Lüdecke HARMS Malchin – DDR 1667–1703
252		Johan SCHÜNEMANN Celle – D 1665–1692
253		Carl FRANTZ Gdańsk – PL M 1673
254		Johann Adolph MEESE Hamburg / Altona – D M 1760
255		Peter Jacob EPLER Hamburg / Altona – D M 1739 † 1759
256		Master J S Kingissep – SU 17th cent.
257		Michael OTTERER Riga – SU B 1603–1646
258		Master P N Tartu – SU 16th cent.
259		Master I N Tartu – SU 16th cent.

LEGENDS

260		Lajos SALTZER Miskolc – H 1826–1877

261 GRIMES	GRIMES & SON London – GB 1817
262 Riedel.	Anton RIEDEL Legnica – PL second third of 19th cent.
263 A JENNER	Anthony JENNER London – GB third quarter of 18th cent.
264 ILLGEN	Ernst August ILLGEN Lubań – PL M 1830 (?)
265 1730L LANGWORTHY	Lawrence LANGWORTHY Newport USA 1730–1739
266 LUDEWIGSLUST	LUDWIGSLUST – D
267 J & H. WARDROP	J. & H. WARDROP Glasgow – GB 1800–1840
268 I.A.EYLERS.	Johann Anton EYLERS Riga – SU 1822 † 1835
269 Thoma.	Georg Heinrich THOMA Hainichen – DDR second third of 19th cent.
270 I.WINCKLER	Joseph WINCKLER Linz – A M 1765 † 1775

271	JOH. RABENBERG · DETERN ·	Johann RABENBERG Detern – D M 1842
272	MALMOUCHE AU MANS	Pierre MALMOUCHE Le Mans – F 1747
273	KOZAK IN·RAAB	KOZÁK Györ – H middle of 19th cent.
274	Jacob Stad	JAKOBSTAD – SF
275	A.W.SCHMELCKE IN HAMBURG	August Wilhelm SCHMELCKE Hamburg – D M 1844
276	I·BENHAM WIGMORE ST	J. BENHAM London – GB c. 1840
277	LIEDEMANN & GÜNTHER KÖNIGSBERG	Johan Ferdinand LIEDEMANN & Friedrich Albert GÜNTHER Kaliningrad – SU M 1858
278	RIGOLIER A PARIS	RIGOLIER Paris – F 1825–1830
279	HENRY·WILL NEW YORK	Henry WILL New York and Albany – USA 1761–1793
280	L.PURCELL BACK·LANE	Laurence PURCELL Dublin – IRL middle of 19th cent.

281		Silvester SAVAGE Dublin – IRL 1788–1827
282		John SHAW Newcastle – GB 1760–1778
283		Catherine DREPTIN Cambrai – F 1830–1840
284		Nicholas SHEPHARD Barnstaple – GB 18th cent.
285		John SHOREY Jr. London – GB middle of 18th cent.
286		Mathew TONKIN London – GB c. middle of 18th cent.
287		HOWEKRING Tartu – SU M 1753 (?) – 1771
288		Hermann Wilhelm PETERSEN Tallinn – SU B 1767 † 1798
289		Samuel HAMLIN Providence – USA 1771–1801
290		James BANCKS Wigan – GB middle of 18th cent.

291		Roger FORD Dublin – IRL c. middle of 18th cent.
292		Anthony KING Dublin – IRL c. middle of 18th cent.
293		Christopher ROBINSON Dublin – IRL † 1759
294		WATTS & HARTON London – GB c. 1810–1860
295		James YATES Birmingham – GB 1800–1840
296		Georg Friedrich BRAUN Györ – H 1802 – 1825
297		Carl GLAUCHE Miskolc – H 1835–1842
298		KINNIBURGH & SON Edinburgh – GB 1826
299		James SHIRLEY Dublin – IRL 1818–1840
300		Samuel GREEN Boston – USA 1779–1828

301		William MACKENZIE London – GB end of 18th cent.
302		Andrew THOMPSON Albany – USA 1811–1817
303		CAMPBELL & CO Belfast – GB middle of 19th cent.
304		David GOURLAY Edinburgh – GB c. 1800
305		Adam RAMAGE Edinburgh – GB middle of 19th cent.
306		John HOGG Paisley – GB 18th cent.
307		Pierre PISSAVY Lyons – F 1850
308		SUZU-KA J after 1940
309		Richard YATES London – GB c. 1785
310		GERARDIN & WATSON London – GB first half of 19th cent.

311		Nathaniel AUSTIN Charleston – USA 1763–1807
312		John Boucher MOODY London – GB first half of 19th cent.
313		TEMPLE & REYNOLDS London – GB first half of 19th cent.
314		W. SEYMOUR & SON Cork – IRL beginning of 19th cent.
315		Johann Friedrich Thomas DAHM Hamburg – D M 1820 † 1872
316		Joh. BECKER Cheb – CS first half of 19th cent.
317		William TAYLOR Exeter and Bristol – GB last quarter of 18th cent.
318		J. P. KAYSER & SOHN Oppum bei Krefeld – D firm established in 1885
319		Humbert LECLERC Lille – F 19th cent.
320		Thomas COMPTON London – GB beginning of 19th cent.

321		Martin MERRY Dublin – IRL c. 1825
322	„ORIVIT"	ORIVIT Cologne – D turn of 19th – 20th cent.
323	„OSIRIS" 5 2 9	OSIRIS (W. Scherf & Co.) Nuremberg – D turn of 19th – 20th cent.
324		ORION Nuremberg – D c. 1900
325		*Lübeckische Probe* quality mark corresponding to Lübeck regulations
326		SALINA & CIE Paris – F 1857–1865
327		Master G P Moscow – SU c. 1730
328		Master C M P T Moscow – SU 18th cent.
329		MOSKOV Moscow – SU 18th cent.
330		S. IVANOV Moscow – SU c. 1730

331	М·СЕМЕНЪ ИВАНОВЪ	Semen IVANOV Moscow – SU c. 1756
332	МЦМ ИВАН	Master IVAN Moscow – SU c. 1730
333	GREGORI. BARANOF.	Gregori BARANOF Moscow – SU c. 1775
334	М·ІВАНЪ ОСІПОВЪ	Ivan OSIPOV Moscow – SU 18th cent.
335	М·ЯКОВА ОСІПОВА	Yakov OSIPOV Moscow – SU c. 1750
336	М·ДВДЪ ОСІПОВЪ	David OSIPOV Moscow – SU 1730–1745
337	М.УСТИНЪ ПЕТРОВЪ.	Ustin PETROV Moscow – SU c. 1732
338	М·ІОВЪ·ВА СИЛЬЕВЪ	Iov VASIL'EV Moscow – SU c. 1725
339	М✶МОСК ОВСКОИ	MOSKOVSKOI Moscow – SU 18th cent.
340	М✶ПЕТРЪ✶ ѲЕДОРОВЪ	Petr FEDOROV Moscow – SU c. 1765

341	**М·АНТИПЪ ИВАНОВЪ**	Antip IVANOV Moscow – SU c. 1730
342	**МРАМАНЪ ІВАНОВЪ**	Raman IVANOV Moscow – SU c. 1750
343	**МАНДРЕЯНЪ ЭАХАРОВЪ.**	Andrean SAKHAROV Moscow – SU c. 1742
344	**МСТЕПАНЪ ВАСИЛЬЕВЪ**	Stepan VASIL'EV Moscow – SU 1725
345	**М·ІВАНЬ ІВАНОВЬ**	Ivan IVANOV Moscow – SU 1758–1775
346	**МСТЕПАНЬ ВАСИЛЬЕВЬ**	Stepan VASIL'EV I Moscow – SU c. 1730
347	**МІВАНЪ·МІ ХАІЛОВЪ**	Ivan MIKHAILOV Moscow – SU c. 1795
348	**МПАРФЕНЪ РЕПИНЪ.**	Parfen REPIN Moscow – SU c. 1775
349	**МАНДАРЕИ ЛУКИЯНОВЪ**	Andrei LUKIANOV Moscow – SU c. 1745
350	**М·НІКОЛАИ НІКИФОРОВ**	Nikolai NIKIFOROV Moscow – SU c. 1725

351	МѲЕДОРѢЯЕ НИСОВСКОИ	Fedor YANISOVSKOI Moscow – SU 18th cent.
352	М·ЦІВАНА ЗОТОВА	Ivan ZOTOV Moscow – SU 1775
353	Ц·М·ІВАНЪ ЧЕМЕЗАВЪ	IVAN CHEMEZAV Moscow – SU c. 1785
354	ЦМСТЕПАНЪ ВАСИЛЬЕВЪ	Stepan VASIL'EV III Moscow – SU c. 1745
355	ЦМ·ІЛЬЯ· ІВАНОВЪ	ILYA IVANOV Moscow – SU first quarter of 18th cent.
356	М:ІВАНЪ· СКОБНІКАВЪ	Ivan SKOBNIKOV Moscow – SU c. 1725
357	М·ТИМОФЕИ БОЖЕНОВЪ	Timofei BOZHENOV Moscow – SU c. 1735
358	Ц Е·МА·АЛЕК СѢИЕГОРОВЪ	Alexei YEGOROV Moscow – SU 18th cent.
359	КОЗМА·ЕРМОЛАЕВЪ	Kozma YERMOLAEV Moscow – SU c. 1740

360		Vasilei MAKEEV Moscow – SU c. 1750
361		Vasilei MAKIOV Moscow – SU c. 1725
362		Semen REMEZOV Moscow – SU c. 1765
363		Antip OSIPOV Moscow – SU c. 1765
364		Andrei ANTONOV Moscow – SU 1735–1762
365		Petr TRAFIMOV Moscow – SU c. 1742
366		J. P. MUHLERT Jelgava – SU 1791–1825
367		PETR FEDOROV Moscow – SU c. 1765
368		Master A V G Moscow – SU – c. 1725 (probably the mark of an earlier supervisory master)

369		Master I P Moscow – SU 1741–1762
370		Master A S N Moscow – SU c. 1725
371		Ivan MIKHAILOV Moscow – SU c. 1795
372		Andrei LUKIANOV Moscow – SU c. 1745
373		Yegor IVANOV Moscow – SU c. 1750

X

374		CHAUMETTE Paris – F from 1887
375		George HAYTER Bristol – GB second half of 18th cent.
376		Alexander HAMILTON London – GB first half of 18th cent.
377		Franz DAMBACH Sibiu – R 1835–1855

MAN AND PARTS OF HIS BODY

378 CHOJNA – PL

379 LAUINGEN – D

380 STOCKHOLM – S

381 MUNICH – D

382 TEPLICE – CS

383 Johann Ernst KOEHLER
Husum – D
M 1742   † 1798

384 James EXCELL
London – GB
first half of 18th cent.

385 Jean Baptiste GONIN
Lyons – F
18th cent.

386 Carl Christoph EBERHARD
Heidenheim – D
M 1838   † 1853

387 George SMITH
London – GB
first quarter of 18th cent.

388		Laurent MORANT Lyons – F c. 1700
389		Edmund SHARROCK London – GB second quarter of 18th cent.
390		James BISHOP London – GB first quarter of 18th cent.
391		John GARDNER Edinburgh – GB third quarter of 18th cent.
392		WOOD & MITCHELL London – GB before middle of 18th cent.
393		Thomas MUNDAY London – GB after middle of 18th cent.
394		Georg SCHEYMANN Jelgava – SU M 1735 † 1775
395		Christian HENTZE Eberswalde – DDR M 1740
396		Johann Hinrich Andreas HÜTTMANN Heide – D M 1786 † before 1817
397		Joseph WATSON London – GB first quarter of 18th cent.

398		Richard ALDERWICK London – GB 1775
399		William GIBBS London – GB beginning of 19th cent.
400		Hinrich TIEDEMANN Lübeck – D M 1776 † 1812
401		Daniel Hinrich TIEDEMANN Lübeck – D B 1804 † 1848
402		Jonathan BONKIN London – GB beginning of 18th cent.
403		Johann Heinrich KAYSER Stargard Szczeciński – PL M 1718 † 1762
404		Benedict WIDTMANN Regensburg – D B 1691 † 1739
405		Philipp Friedrich MAIER Reutlingen – D * 1733 † 1786
406		Jeremias BIEDERMANN Wrocław – PL M 1635 † 1673
407		Christian Gottlieb POHLMANN Schwerin – DDR M 1730 † 1766

408		Daniel Gottlob REINHARD Zittau – DDR M 1773 † 1806
409		Hans Wilhelm BOLDT Lübeck – D B 1740 † 1758
410		Carl Friedrich SCHWARZ Glauchau – DDR M 1765 † 1806
411		Joseph HEILLINGÖTTER Karlovy Vary – CS 18th cent.
412		Richard AUSTIN Boston – USA 1793–1817
413		BLAUBEUREN – D
414		Johann Christoffer NEUMANN Bergen a. Rügen– DDR M 1776
415		Abraham KUPFERSCHMIDT Tallinn – SU B 1758–1797
416		John LAFFAR London – GB first quarter of 18th cent.
417		Hinrich Gottfried WELLMANN Hamburg – D M 1777 † 1817

418		Andreas Heinrich MEYER Celle – D B 1731 † 1772
419		Richard BOWLER London – GB after middle of 18th cent.
420		Bartholomew ELLIOT London – GB second quarter of 18th cent.
421		Robert WALLER London – GB last quarter of 18th cent.
422		Johann Adolf GOSSE Pirna – DDR M 1706 † 1758
423		Martin GEISSLER Ścinawa – PL from middle of 18th cent. † 1766
424		Samuel WOODS Waterford – IRL 1820–1840
425		Paul FISHER London – GB 1798 † 1837
426		Edward LAWRENCE London – GB first quarter of 18th cent.
427		Isaac READ London – GB middle of 18th cent.

428		Greenhill LINDSEY London – GB first quarter of 18th cent.
429		James STEEVENS London – GB middle of 18th cent.
430		Robert BUSH & CO. Bristol and Bilton – GB end of 18th cent.
431		Kozma YERMOLAEV Moscow – SU c. 1740
432		Anton Christian BEATHON Stade – D * 1769 † 1855
433		Johann Daniel LANCKHAR Lübeck – D B 1761 † 1782
434		Georg ÖTZMANN Lüneburg – D M 1750 † 1763
435		Alexander STAEHLE Urach – D * 1803 † 1886
436		Carl Wilhelm ROESSLER Bautzen – DDR M 1819–1861
437		Heinrich Burchardt ALSLEBEN Zittau – DDR M 1763 † 1800

438		Otto Friedrich GROTH Brzeg – PL M 1792 † after 1822
439		Balthasar Wilhelm MÜLLER Głogów – PL 1781–1809
440		WURZEN – DDR
441		Hans Conrad SCHNEWLI Stein am Rhein – CH 1734–1768
442		Wilhelm Friedrich JÜRGENSEN Rendsburg – D M 1780
443		HEIDE – D
444		William HOWARD London – GB middle of 18th cent.
445		Peter le KEUX London – GB last quarter of 18th cent.
446		Anton NUSSMANN Marktbreit – D M 1812 † before 1824
447		DZIERŻONIÓW – PL

448		Ernst Mattheus WASSERMANN Ulm – D M 1786 (?) † 1831
449		CURTIS & CO. Bristol – GB c. 1800
450		James CURTIS Bristol – GB 1770–1793
451		P. EDGAR & SON Bristol – GB middle of 19th cent.
452		GRYFÓW ŚLĄSKI – PL
453		FRAUENFELD – CH
454		Johann George ELIAS Kuldiga – SU B 1774 † 1800
455		Friedrich Ferdinand MADAME Freiburg (Brsg.) – D 1735 † 1773
456		T. & W. WILLSHIRE Bristol – GB c. 1800
457		John HINDE London – GB second half of 18th cent.

458		John Gray GREEN London – GB end of 18th cent.
459		Carl Adolph BÖHMER Pirna – DDR M 1823–1860
460		Johann SCHARNING Jr. Kołobrzeg – PL M 1690 † 1731
461		Christian Wilhelm HOHENNER Wunsiedel – D last third of 18th cent. † 1803
462		Baltazar ROKUS Arboga – S 1743–1788
463		Christian WEHLING Jr. Neumünster – D M 1694 (?) † 1773
464		Friedrich Ernst FINCK Güstrow – DDR M 1757 † 1797
465		Johann Jacob FINCK Güstrow – DDR M 1798 † 1831
466		Jochim Jacob KRUMBÜGEL Güstrow – DDR M 1774 † after 1830
467		Hans KRETSCHMER Świdnica – PL M 1672 † 1715

468		Wilhelm Gotth. FISCHER Prenzlau – DDR M 1803
469		Johann Christoph SCHULTZ Havelberg – DDR M 1801
470		Hans POPSEN Tønder – DK M 1721
471		Peter SCHERFFENBERG Flensburg – D M 1734
472		HEIDE – D
473		Georg KLOSE Opava – CS † 1690
474		Johann George WILDNER Dzierżoniów – PL M 1732 (?) † 1768
475		Tiedemann Hinrich STELLING Hamburg – D M 1789 † 1815
476		Johann Gottlob ROESLER Zittau – DDR M 1773 † 1802
477		Johann Albertus SCHULTZE Wrocław – PL B 1735 † 1770

478		Carl Friedrich LOTH Plauen – DDR B 1752 † 1806
479		Friedrich Menzo PULß Oleśnica – PL M 1718 (?) † before 1761
480		George Christlieb ASSMANN Altenberg – DDR M 1740 † 1771
481		Christian Gotthold SCHERFIG Zwickau – DDR M 1780
482		Michael KAYSER Riga – SU B 1715 † 1760
483		Christoph BERGER Brzeg – PL M 1727 † 1746
484		Carl Gottlieb NEUMANN Dresden – DDR M 1774 † 1795
485		Melchior Friedrich NIERÖSE Gorzów Wielkopolski – PL M 1735 † 1769
486		Master M M Prešov – CS c. 1700
487		GLÜCKSTADT – D

488	Master C S Tallinn – SU first half of 18th cent.
489	Gottlieb Leberecht KRAEFT I Hamburg / Altona – D M 1756–1802
490	Master C L Jelgava – SU 1829–1835
491	Johann Gottlob FLACH Eibenstock – DDR M before 1763 † c. 1789
492	Johann Gottfried GROSSMANN Bautzen – DDR M 1775
493	Rosina HAHN (widow of Tobias Hahn) Legnica – PL (mark from 1720)
494	Master D P R Košice – CS 18th cent.
495	Christian Ludwig BEINDORF Frankfurt a. M. – D first third of 19th cent. † 1836
496	Christoph WALDNER Mulhouse – F 1757–1827
497	Johann BAPTIST Jr. (?) Mainz – D 1874–1891

498		Johann Christian IBERT Strzelin – PL M 1751 (?) † 1805
499		Hans Rudolf MANZ Zürich – CH * 1771 † 1829
500		Johann Georg NEEFF Frankfurt a. M. – D M 1770 † 1802
501		Johann Siegfried METZEL Wittstock – DDR M 1772
502		Johann George STIER Tallinn – SU B 1720 † 1767
503		Johann Carl Daniel SAEDLER Tartu – SU B 1789 † 1810
504		Martin RUCKERT Würzburg – D M 1821–1853
505		Ludwig FELDMETH Karlsruhe – D M 1817 † 1869
506		Jacques Frédéric BORST Strasbourg – F 1769–1810
507		Johann Ernst RAEDER Gorzów Wielkopolski – PL M 1779–1798

508		Christian August THIEME Karl-Marx-Stadt – DDR M 1776 – beginning of 19th cent.
509		Johann Gottfried GEELHAAR Meissen – DDR M 1781–1810
510		BRANDMÜLLER Aschaffenburg – D from 1898
511		Abraham KUPFERSCHMIDT Tallinn – SU M 1758–1797
512		George STIER Tallinn – SU M 1763 † 1781
513		Hermann Wilhelm PETERSEN Tallinn – SU B 1767 † 1798
514		HOWEKRING Tartu – SU M 1753 (?) – 1771
515		Johann Sebastian STIER Tallinn – SU M 1744 † 1779
516		Peter WITTORF Hamburg – D M 1843 † 1878

517		Georg Friedrich BRAUN Györ – H 1802–1825
518		Dietrich Jacob TRIPPE Soest – D † 1786
519		Johann FAUSER Budapest – H M 1805
520		Johann Baptist FINCK Sen. Mainz – D third quarter of 19th cent.
521		Andreas WIRZ II Zürich – CH * 1767 † 1813
522		Joseph NEIDHARDT Horní Slavkov – CS first half of 19th cent.
523		Friedrich PELET Kaliningrad – SU M 1798 (mark used from 1810)
524		Johann WERLIN Marburg – D * 1752 † 1799
525		Johann Gottfried FRISCH Marburg – D M 1767 (?) † 1797

526		Gottfried STENZEL Jelgava – U M 1770 † 1795
527		Johann Wilhelm FELDTMAN Jelgava – SU 1795–1826
528		Gottfried MARTINI Liepaja – SU 1756
529		Johannes Jonas WERLIN Marburg – D M 1732 (?) † 1790
530		Benjamin FALCK Pärnu – SU 1783 † 1808
531		Johann Gottfried Wilhelm FRIESENDORFF Jelgava – SU 1769–1794
532		Vasilii SKVARTSOV Moscow – SU c. 1765
533		Gregori BARANOF Moscow – SU c. 1775
534		Joh. Matthäus WERLIN Marburg – D M 1744 † 1777

535		Joh. Jacob ISENHEIM Strasbourg – F M 1762 † 1797
536		Johann Matthias AICHINGER Weiden – D B 1834 † 1884
537		Christian KRÄMER Marburg – D M 1800 † 1849
538		Christian Ludwig BEINDORF Frankfurt a. M. – D first third of 19th cent. † 1836
539		Anton Ludwig SEIDEL Marburg – D M 1830 † c. 1865
540		Arthur CHAUMETTE Paris – F from 1887
541		Johann Conrad GRÜNEWALD Bayreuth – D M 1816 (?) † 1862
542		Georg Nicolas ZEITLER Bayreuth – D M 1844
543		Johann Gerhard ECKHOLT Haselünne – D * 1808 – second third of 19th cent.

544		R. MEYER Jelgava – SU – 1862
545		John JONES Jr. London – GB † 1783
546		Hermann Adrian STRÜVE Osnabrück – D 1716 † 1758
547		Joseph LUTZ Česká Lípa – CS M 1795
548		Johann Wilhelm PLAGEMANN Hamburg / Altona – D M 1820 † 1859
549		Christian KRÄMER Marburg – D M 1800 † 1849
550		Master B I Grobinya – SU 1703
551		Friedrich Christian PETERS Varel – D * 1828 † 1882
552		Philippus GÖRDES Soest – D second half of 18th cent.
553		Johann Diedrich SIEFKEN Westerstede – D first half of 19th cent.

554	Niklaus UEBELIN II Basel – CH first half of 18th cent. † 1756
555	Philippe DOLFUS Mulhouse – F 1718–1754
556	Carl Georg BÜTTNER Hamburg / Altona – D M 1781
557	Christian Bitter THIER Dortmund – D 1763
558	Carl VOIGT Oldenburg – D M 1809 † 1865
559	Johann Christian MECKSEPER Hamburg – D M 1738
560	Lübbert Diedrich BAHLMANN Quakenbrück – D * 1710 – third quarter of 18th cent.
561	Richard BACHE London – GB last quarter of 18th – be- ginning of 19th cent.
562	Johann Jürgen Christoph SOMMER Hamburg – D M 1768 † 1797

563		Johann Jochim RIECK Hamburg / Altona – D M 1744
564		Claus Peter SCHWEEN Hamburg / Altona – D M 1831
565		Johann LÜDERS Hamburg – D M 1740 † before 1771
566		Adam Heinrich LUKAFFSKY Jelgava – SU 1757–1779
567		Anton Rudolph REGELER Hamburg / Altona – D B 1757
568		Daniel SCHUBERT Angermünde – DDR M 1706
569		Jacob Frantz FOX Braniewo – PL M 1800
570		Heinrich Cornelius Martin HAGELSTEIN Hamburg – D M 1828 † 1845
571		Georg Lambert Matthias GRAVE Hamburg – D * 1767 † before 1792

572		Andreas Goswin JOCKENACK Dortmund – D 1724–1775
573		Peter Heinrich HEISING Bielefeld – D c. 1780
574		Johann HAYEN III Riga – SU M 1772 † 1821
575		KUTNÁ HORA – CS
576		Gabriel SYREN Frankfurt a. M. – D M 1727
577		György TRILLHAS Miskolc – H 1800–1844
578		Joseph Andreas ZAMPONI II Leoben – A M 1792 † 1837
579		Friedrich KEGEMANN Soest – D 1809 † 1816
580		Abraham KUPFERSCHMIDT Tallinn – SU 1758–1797

581	John KING London – GB second half of 18th cent.
582	Michael SCHÜTT Jr. Elmshorn – D M 1765
583	John DAVIS London – GB first half of 18th cent.
584	Max HEDIGER Zürich – CH from 1851
585	Caspar Heinrich TIARKS Jever – D B 1797 † 1843
586	Johann Hinrich TIARKS I Jever – D * 1723 † 1804
587	Johann Wilhelm WAGENER Esens – D M 1795 † 1821
588	Wesel Joseph BRINKMANN Cloppenburg – D * 1779 † 1862
589	Hans Michelsen SPERLING Copenhagen – DK M 1782
590	Jacob Conrad BOHNEKAMP Neustadtgödens – D first half of 19th cent.

591		Jan KLINT Leer – D * 1800–1872
592		Johannes Jansen KANNENGIEßER Esens – D * 1724–1779
593		Wilhelm Henrich THIER Dortmund – D * 1767 † 1822
594		Eberhard TREMBLAU Menden – D 1807 † 1843
595		Borchart WALDIS Riga – SU M 1526–1536 † 1557
596		MUNICH – D 17th cent.
597		MUNICH – D
598		LINDKÖPING – S
599		Johann Michael THOMAS Pärnu – SU B 1751–1761
600		François LAINÉ Paris – F M 1736

601		Robert PATIENCE London – GB second third of 18th cent. – 1777
602		REICHENBACH – DDR
603		Stephan LOIBL Budapest – H 1768–1787 (mark used from 1782)
604		Tomáš RIXY Prague / Malá Strana – CS M 1760
605		I. A. SCHIRSAND Karlovy Vary – CS 18th cent.
606		Samuel KNIGHT London – GB beginning of 18th cent.
607		John HEANEY Dublin – IRL second half of 18th cent.
608		Henry IRVING London – GB 1750
609		Pierre MARTIN Paris – F 1720

610		Adam Gottlieb SPIESS Szprotawa – PL 1786 † 1821
611		Isaac FAUST Strasbourg – F 1623–1669
612		Johann Michael EMMERICH Strasbourg – F M 1705 † 1753
613		Johann Carl SPIESS Zagań – PL M 1778 † 1802
614		Hermann Daniel MEYER Lübeck – D B 1782–1823
615		NORRKÖPING – S
616		Abraham KUPFERSCHMIDT Tallinn – SU 1758–1797
617		Nils Christophersson FORSS Västerås – S 1740–1786
618		Johann Hinrich von BREMEN Ploen – D M 1717 (?) † 1761
619		Daniel LAWSON London – GB c. middle of 18th cent.

620		John EWEN London – GB after 1700
621		David BUDDEN London – GB beginning of 18th cent.
622		James PULESTON London – GB middle of 18th cent.
623		Joseph DONNE London – GB second quarter of 18th cent.
624		MEDIAŞ – R
625		SCHWÄBISCH HALL – D
626		Traugott Friedrich August PILZ Freiberg – DDR M 1811–1843
627		William HANDY London – GB 18th cent.
628		James EVERETT London – GB first half of 18th cent.
629		Pierre LAPLACE Château-du-Loir – F 1691

630		James EVERETT Philadelphia – USA 1716–1717
631		Mark of the Tsar's Court Moscow – SU
632		Semen REMEZOV Moscow – SU c. 1765
633		Bourchier & Richard CLEEVE London – GB c. 1754
634		Thomas PHILLIPS London – GB from end of 18th cent. † 1849
635		John WARNE London – GB end of 18th cent.
636		BURGUM & CATCOTT Bristol and Littledean, Glos. – GB c. 1765
637		M. FOTHERGILL & SONS Bristol – GB end of 18th cent.
638		William HITCHINS London – GB second half of 18th cent. (the date in the mark probably indicates establishment of a firm of the same name)
639		Thomas SCATTERGOOD London – GB — 18th cent.

ANIMALS

640		WASSERBURG a. Inn – D
641		HARBURG a. d. Elbe – D
642		GRAZ – A
643		GRAZ – A
644		STEYER – A
645		PEGAU – DDR
646		MITTWEIDA – DDR
647		KŁODZKO – PL
648		STEYER – A
649		HORNÍ SLAVKOV – CS 17th cent.

650		KARL-MARX-STADT – DDR
651		FREIBERG – DDR
652		GÖRLITZ – DDR
653		GÖRLITZ – DDR
654		LÖBAU – DDR
655		SAYDA – DDR
656		OSCHATZ – DDR
657		AUERBACH – DDR
658		Joseph SEIFF Wasserburg a. Inn – D B 1795–1818
659		OELSNITZ – DDR

660		Magnus SÖDERBERG Stockholm – S M 1716–1748
661		LEONBERG – D after 1705
662		LÜNEBURG – D
663		Thomas DANFORTH Stepney, Connecticut and Philadelphia, Pennsylvania – USA 1777–1818
664		Franz HÖFLER Passau – D 1784–1816
665		Johann Friedrich SPEISER Kirchheim – D * 1803 † 1882
666		Hans Friedrich LÖWE Kiel – D M 1761 † 1806
667		Christian CATHREIN Amöneburg – D c. 1789 † 1855
668		Peter Hinrich LÖWE Kiel – D M 1803 † 1848
669		Philip WHITE London – GB last quarter of 18th cent.

670		André DULAC Le Puy-en-Velay – F c. 1750
671		Antoine FANON Lyons – F 18th cent.
672		Joseph RABAYET Clermont-Ferrand – F end of 18th cent.
673		John HOSKYN Truro – GB c. 1750
674		Rollin GREFFET Lyons – F second third of 16th cent.
675		Daubeny TURBERVILLE London – GB first half of 18th cent.
676		Philip ROBERTS London – GB second third of 18th cent.
677		CAMBRAI – F
678		E. DREPTIN Cambrai – F 19th cent.
679		Jean CHABROL Lyons – F after 1643

680		Nathaniel AUSTIN Charleston – USA 1763–1807
681		John DANFORTH Norwich – USA 1773–1793
682		Thomas DANFORTH II Middletown – USA 1755–1782
683		Joseph DANFORTH Middletown – USA 1780–1788
684		Gershom JONES Providence – USA 1774–1809
685		William COOK Bristol and Gloucester – GB end of 18th – beginning of 19th cent.
686		Thomas BENNET Bristol and English Bicknor, Glos. – GB second half of 18th cent.
687		John HARRISON York – GB first half of 18th cent.
688		John WYNN London – GB third quarter of 18th cent.

689		Thomas PARKER London – GB end of 17th cent.
690		Robert HITCHMAN London – GB second third of 18th cent.
691		John SKINNER Boston – USA 1760–1790
692		John OSBORNE London – GB first half of 18th cent.
693		GÖTEBORG – S
694		LIEPAJA – SU
695		KÖNIGSTEIN – DDR
696		Paul BARTH Jr. Wrocław – PL M 1640 † 1655
697		Johann Joseph BEYER Nysa – PL M 1725 † 1741
698		Bernhard GULIELMINETTI Kitzbühel – A 1788–1827

699		Carl Frederik TREYER Uppsala – S 1752–1769
700		Philip GILCH Prague / Nové Město – CS M 1773 † 1798
701		Thomas LAUW Meldorf – D M 1758 * 1773
702		LEGNICA – PL
703		John KENT London – GB 1718–1759
704		HORNÍ SLAVKOV – CS 18th cent.
705		Sigismund Gottlieb BÖHM Świdnica – PL B 1728 † 1774
706		ADORF – DDR
707		Anton Jeremias GÖTZ II Děčín – CS M 1740

708		KARLSHAMM – S
709		Edward HOLMAN London – GB end of 17th cent.
710		Imanuel Siegesmund **BAESTLEIN** Döbeln – D M 1799 † 1851
711		BIBERACH – D
712		LAVEUR Paris – F 1909–1958
713		UPPSALA – S
714		John BOTELER London – GB c. middle of 18th cent.
715		Robert MORSE London – GB beginning of 18th cent.
716		Joseph AUSTEN & SON Cork – IRL 1823–1833
717		IRON MUNSTER CO. Cork – IRL 1833–1905

718		William BEAMONT London – GB beginning of 18th cent.
719		Richard NORFOLK London – GB 1736 – † 1783
720		William RICH Bristol – GB c. 1840
721		BERGEN auf Rügen – DDR
722		ENNS – A
723		Christoph REICHENBERGER Amberg – D B 1652
724		EGGENFELDEN – D
725		VESOUL – F
726		KARLOVY VARY – CS
727		Christoph Ignatius JAIS Tölz – D M 1771

728		Thomas BENNET London – GB 1700
729		Sir George ALDERSON London – GB first quarter of 19th cent. † 1826
730		KARLOVY VARY – CS
731		VILSHOFEN – D
732		BAYREUTH – D
733		WINTERTHUR – CH
734		PIRNA – DDR
735		GROSSENHAIN – DDR
736		Henry WOOD London – GB second half of 18th cent.
737		A. CARTER London – GB c. 1750

738		Robert SEATCHARD London — GB after middle of 18th cent. † 1766
739		SCHEIBENBERG — DDR
740		GRYFÓW ŚLĄSKI — PL
741		GREIFSWALD — DDR
742		RIBNITZ — DDR
743		Claes Eric HELAND Norrköping — S 1766–1784
744		Heinrich Frantz LANGER Nysa — PL M 1716–1721
745		WOLGAST — DDR
746		YSTAD — S
747		Christian Hinrich GRÄPCKE Hamburg — D B 1721

748	Hans Christian GRÄPCKE Hamburg – D M 1746–1783
749	Mattheus BINNER Wrocław – PL M 1694 † 1756
750	Johann Martin REITMAYR Traunstein – D M 1722 (?) † 1770
751	William Sandys GREEN London – GB first half of 18th cent.
752	Joseph MONK London – GB third quarter of 18th cent.
753	George GREENFELL London – GB third quarter of 18th cent.
754	John GRIFFITH Bristol – GB † 1755
755	Robert BUSH Senr. Bristol and Bilton, Glos. – GB second half of 18th cent.
756	Simon HALFORD London – GB first half of 18th cent.
757	VENICE – I 15th cent.

758		William COWLING London – GB after – 1737
759		Thomas PAGE Bristol – GB first half of 18th cent.
760		SŁUPSK – PL
761		SŁUPSK – PL
762		GIENGEN – D
763		Johann Christoph MILLER Schwäbisch Gmünd – D M 1740
764		Benedikt KAMMERER Schwäbisch Gmünd – D * 1812 † 1870
765		Joseph FOSTER London – GB second half of 18th cent.
766		John SELLON London – GB c. middle of 18th cent.
767		Thomas BARNES London – GB second quarter of 18th cent.

768		Thomas **BOULTON** Wigan – GB c. 1750
769		William **COOCH** London – GB after 1775
770		**SCHLEIZ – DDR**
771		Johann Sebastian **STIER** Tallinn – SU M 1744 † 1779
772		Johann Georg **RÜCKERT** Ochsenfurt – D 18th cent.
773		**SEDAN – F**
774		**GÜSTROW – DDR**
775		F. **BECHLIN** Güstrow – DDR M 1841
776		John **COLE** London – GB c. 1727
777		**FREISING – D**

778		James FONTAIN London – GB second half of 18th cent.
779		John GURNELL London – GB second half of 18th cent.
780		Carl WESMAN Stockholm – S 1757–1772
781		Carl LOGREN Falun – S 1750–1775
782		John BROWN London – GB from end of 18th cent. † 1836
783		Gideon SCHMIDT Tallinn – SU B 1647 – 1682
784		ROSSWEIN – DDR
785		STUTTGART – D
786		Christian Friedrich HOHENSTEIN Döbeln – D M 1747 † 1765
787		Eberhardt VAHLE Celle – D B 1737 † 1755

788
Heinrich Ernst SCHRÖDER
Celle – D
M 1776 † 1813

789
Rudolph VAHLE
Celle – D
M 1765 † 1775

790
Jacob Christoph VAHLE
Celle – D
M 1760, leaves C. in 1767
† 1776

791
SCHMIEDEBERG – DDR

792
Georg Heinrich MÜLLER
Celle – D
M 1767 † 1804

793
Johann Peter Wilhelm
MÜLLER
Celle – D
B 1807 † 1811

794
Carl KRÜGER
Racibórz – PL
B 1846 † 1888

795
Richard LEGATT
London – GB
1722

796

John EDWARDS
London – GB
second third of 18th cent.

797		Andries MICHEL New York – USA c. 1742–1752
798		EGLISAU – CH
799		JELENIA GÓRA – PL
800		Anton MESCHEDER Dzierżoniów – PL M c. 1788 † 1802
801		Johann Carl AGRATH Nysa – PL M 1683 (?) † 1704
802		Carl Paul HIBLER Rosenheim – D M 1755 (?) † 1820
803		Carl August SEYBOLD Grossenhain – DDR M 1765
804		Paul Friedrich EBERT I Auerbach – DDR M 1759 † 1800
805		Johann George HEGEWALDT Jr. Leipzig – DDR M 1749 † 1772
806		Conrad KREIDE Wriezen – DDR M 1779

807		Johann Hartmann WOLTER Friedland – DDR M 1770
808		Gerhard WOHLERS Mölln – D M 1754 † 1780
809		M. COUSTARD Angers – F M 1640
810		JELENIA GÓRA – PL
811		L. H. SCHWEDER Güstrow – DDR M 1740 † 1764
812		John UBLY London – GB c. middle of 18th cent.
813		Philip ROGERS London – GB beginning of 18th cent.
814		Jonathan BRODHURST London – GB first quarter of 18th cent.
815		Caspar ECKE Sen. Szczecin – PL M 1631 † 1667

816		ROUEN – F
817		Christoph RÜHLE Meissen – DDR M 1709 † 1742
818		SÖDERKÖPING – S
819		Gottlieb HILSCHER Wrocław – PL B 1712 † 1735
820		George KRISCHE Wrocław – PL M 1638 † 1678
821		Johan BRUHN Västervik – S 1778–1789
822		Robert CROOKE London – GB after 1738
823		Jacob Heinrich WEISS Schneeberg – DDR M 1827 † 1882
824		Claus Christoph BUBERT Lübeck – D B 1778 † 1792
825		Eric BJÖRKMAN Stockholm – S 1741–1761

826	Ezechiáš F. RISSPLER Prague / Staré Město – CS M 1685 † 1713
827	Johann Andreas DOERFFEL Nysa – PL M 1726 † 1774
828	Johann Christian KOCHAUF Linz – A M c. 1746 † 1771
829	Johann Gottfried ROTHE Leipzig – DDR M 1736 † 1789
830	Johann Gottlieb SCHROT Jr. Grimma – DDR M 1749
831	Johan Henrik BODECKER Karlskrona – S 1758–1785
832	Hinrich Diedrich LEMPF Buxtehude – D last quarter of 18th cent.
833	Michael Gottlob WÖLFEL Bautzen – DDR M 1752 † 1784
834	Johann Jacob von FÜHREN Nysa – PL M 1691 † 1726
835	Thomas HODGE Tiverton – GB c. 1720–1750

836		CHERCHIN Evreux – F 1742
837		Kaspar MATTON Karlovy Vary – CS c. 1800
838		Richard GOING Bristol – GB 18th cent.
839		William J. ELSWORTH New York – USA 1767–1798
840		John VAUGHAN London – GB second half of 18th cent. † 1807
841		Charles JONES London – GB end of 18th cent.
842		Samuel ELLIS London – GB middle of 18th cent. † 1773
843		Samuel BILLING Coventry – GB c. 1675 † 1707
844		LEVEAU Paris – F 1815–1840

845		Abraham LEMCKE Elbląg – PL M 1701
846		Jacob MANSRIEDER Linz – A M 1683 † 1724
847		Hieronymus LEDERMAYR Wels – A M 1628 † after 1669
848		James HUGHES London – GB end of 17th cent.
849		HÄRNÖSAND – S
850		Johann Philipp VOLCKMAR Siegen – D from 1763
851		VARIDO Paris – F 1909–1958
852		Johann Nicolaus REDER Stralsund – DDR B 1763 † 1818
853		WOOD & HILL London – GB end of 18th cent.
854		PITT & DADLEY London – GB end of 18th cent.

855		**PRITZWALK – DDR**
856		**TOWNSEND & GRIFFIN** London – GB 1777–1801
857		William James **ENGLEFIELD** London – GB end of 19th – beginning of 20th cent.
858		**GAULS** Exeter – GB c. 1810
859		**TOWNSEND & COMPTON** London – GB 1801–1811
860		John **TOWNSEND** London – GB second half of 18th cent.
861		Richard **AUSTIN** Boston – USA 1793–1817
862		Thomas **COMPTON** & **TOWNSEND** London – GB c. 1801–1817
863		**ARRAS – F**

864		ERMATINGEN – CH
865		STECKBORN – CH
866		WIL – CH
867		BERLIN – Germany
868		Abraham GANTING Bern – CH second third of 18th cent.
869		Johann Paul Carl ARNOLD Mainbernheim – D M 1778 beginning of 19th cent.
870		Thomas HOPKINS London – GB after 1700
871		UELZEN – D
872		LIEPAJA – SU
873		VARBERG – S

874		John HOME London – GB third quarter of 18th cent.
875		Nathaniel BARBER London – GB last third of 18th cent.
876		ŚWIDNICA – PL
877		EBERSWALDE – DDR
878		Peter GRÜNEWALD Sen. Greifswald – DDR M 1669
879		George HESSLER Wrocław – PL M 1632/3 † 1660
880		Andreas HAAS Kulmbach – D M 1690 (?)
881		Edward LEAPIDGE London – GB first half of 18th cent.
882		Thomas JAMES London – GB first half of 18th cent.
883		JIHLAVA – CS

884		William BRAINE London – GB c. 1680
885		Joseph HENRY London – GB 18th cent.
886		John ROLT London – GB first quarter of 18th cent.
887		Francis HUDSON York – GB after middle of 18th cent.
888		ÖSTHAMMAR – S
889		Jochim HECHT Rostock – DDR M 1780 † 1812
890		NARVA – SU
891		Ralph HULL London – GB last quarter of 18th cent.
892		FLY & THOMPSON London – GB first half of 18th cent.
893		Aquila DACKOMBE London – GB c. middle of 18th cent.

894		REHNA – DDR
895		URI – CH
896		STRELITZ – DDR
897		KONITZ – DDR
898		MALCHIN – DDR
899		TETEROW – DDR
900		SCHAFFHAUSEN – CH
901		François VAUDRY Paris – F 1778
902		HUDIKSVALL – S
903		LINKÖPING – S

904		HOF a. d. Saale — D
905		John CATER London – GB 18th cent.
906		William WRIGHT London – GB second half of 18th cent.
907		Charles CLARKE Waterford – IRL 1790–1810
908		Rice BROOKS London – GB 1667
909		Thomas BUCKBY London – GB first half of 18th cent.
910		John WILLIAMS London – GB first half of 18th cent.
911		Richard YATES London – GB 1772 – beginning of 19th cent.
912		William HARRIS London – GB c. middle of 18th cent.
913		William WHITE London – GB second half of 18th cent.

914		Ralph WHARRAM London – GB second half of 18th cent.
915		BIRCH & VILLERS Birmingham – GB 1775–1820
916		Stephen COX Bristol – GB † 1754
917		Nathaniel BESSANT London – GB beginning of 18th cent.
918		Samuel DUNCOMB Birmingham – GB 1740–1775 (?)
919		RÖBEL – DDR
920		GADEBUSCH – DDR
921		GNOIEN – DDR
922		WROCŁAV / LEŚNICA – PL

923		STERNBERG – DDR
924		Johann Alexander OECHSLIN Schaffhausen – CH * 1823 † 1870
925		Johann Conrad SCHALCH IV Schaffhausen – CH * 1801 † 1849
926		WITTENBERG – DDR
927		PRICHSENSTADT – D
928		OSTERHOFEN – D
929		JELGAVA – SU
930		GÖPPINGEN – D
931		Johan Georg BERNER Göppingen – D * 1796 † 1853
932		JELGAVA – SU

933		Christoph Friedrich KALLENBERG Sen. Winnenden – D M 1829 † 1864
934		Gottlob Friedrich BOECKMANN Tübingen – D M 1837 (?) † 1874

BIRDS

935		Hans Jürgen LIEBLER Liepaja – SU 1670–1694 (?)
936		Claus KAHNS Malchin – DDR M 1712 † c. 1744
937		Christian ROHRLACH Wrocław – PL last quarter of 17th cent. † 1710
938		Johann Gottlieb BLASIUS Leipzig – DDR M 1733 † 1774
939		Christian Gottlieb SCHUBERT Bierutów – PL M 1735
940		Andreas Christoph BECHERER Marburg – D * 1781 † 1821
941		Adam Samuel TRÄNCKNER Dresden – DDR M 1742 † 1772
942		Johann Peter REIMPEL Gadebusch – DDR M 1738 † 1777

943		Thomas WILLSHIRE Bristol – GB end of 18th cent.
944		GRAÝ & KING London – GB first half of 18th cent.
945		OLEŚNICA – PL
946		Georg Christoph MAAS Nysa – PL M 1703 (?) † 1720
947		Samuel Traugott RABE Lwówek Śląski – PL 1783
948		Benjamin Gottlob EBERT Świdnica – PL B 1742 † 1794
949		C. H. KINTZEL Świdnica – PL M 1830–1845
950		Johann Peter HÖNERLAH Hamburg / Harburg – D M 1781 † 1828
951		Robert BALDWIN Wigan – GB c. 1690–1726
952		Edward SEAWELL London – GB last quarter of 18th cent.

953		Christian Diederich **HINTZPETER** Hamburg / Altona – D M 1792 † 1833
954		Conrad Ludwig **STEINHARDT** Stuttgart – D M 1755 † 1798
955		John ORMISTON Dublin – IRL last third of 18th cent.
956		LEOBEN – A
957		Peter GILLMAN Stockholm – S 1770–1798
958		William NETTLEFOLD London – GB turn of 18th – 19th cent.
959		Gottfried KUGELLMANN Szczecin – PL B 1773
960		Vicenz BUREL Steyer – A M 1626
961		Johann Gottlieb **MÜSSIGGANG** Bautzen – DDR M 1710 † 1751
962		Christian Heinrich VOGEL Schneeberg – DDR M 1769 † 1822

963		Johan Heinrich OHRDORF Celle – D M 1727 † 1751
964		Benjamin Gottlieb LANGE Wrocław – PL M 1763 † 1798
965		Benjamin Heinrich GOTTESPFENNIG Rostock – DDR M 1747
966		Johann Gottlieb GENSCH Sen. Wrocław – PL M 1747 † 1790
967		Benedict PRELL Legnica – PL * 1716 (?) † 1787
968		ZŁOTORYJA – PL
969		Johann Caspar KOEPCKE Itzehoe – D M 1756 † 1796
970		George Friedrich SPEER Ścinawa – PL M c. 1714 † 1746
971		William KIRBY New York – USA 1760–1793
972		Thomas RHODES London – GB first half of 18th cent.

973		Matthias KÜHN Słupsk – PL B 1757
974		Carl August Wilhelm DÖRFLIG Dresden – DDR M 1846 † 1881
975		William Harrison KING London – GB 18th cent.
976		Thomas BATTESON London – GB second half of 17th cent.
977		Johann Friedrich LEMFF Schwerin – DDR M 1737 † 1755
978		Bartolomaeus STIETE Zittau – DDR M 1736 † 1766
979		Carl Moritz DAMM Rochlitz – DDR M 1804
980		Valentin Anton LIPP Eggenfelden – D M c. 1756 † 1810
981		M. ROLLET Dijon – F 1743
982		Jean GRAVES Bordeaux – F 1683–1727

983		Edmund HARVEY GB or IRL c. 1700–1750
984		Martin MEUNIER Lille – F 19th cent.
985		FRANKFURT a. d. O. – DDR
986		Benjamin PARHAM Plymouth – GB c. 1725
987		Henry LITTLE London – GB second third of 18th cent.
988		Samuel RIGHTON London – GB c. 1732–1743
989		Joseph PEDDER London – GB first half of 18th cent.
990		Samuel SPATEMAN London – GB † 1768
991		Roger PYE London – GB c. 1740
992		Samuel COCKS London – GB beginning of 19th cent.

993		Richard COLLIER London – GB beginning of 18th cent.
994		John HUDSON London – GB turn of 18th–19th cent. † 1829
995		ZWICKAU – DDR
996		Charles William LOADER London – GB end of 18th cent.
997		Robert SADLER Newcastle – GB 1730–1780
998		William HOGG Newcastle – GB c. 1760–1795
999		Norton PARR Cork – IRL † 1773
1000		Thomas GOSLING London – GB first quarter of 18th cent.
1001		Charles Puckle MAXEY London – GB c. middle of 18th cent.
1002		Robert PORTEOUS London – GB second half of 18th cent.

1003		John KENRICK London – GB c. middle of 18th cent.
1004		Alexander LANCASTER London – GB first quarter of 18th cent.
1005		Alexander HAMPHIE Dublin – IRL 1719
1006		Richard WRIGHT London – GB first quarter of 18th cent.
1007		Richard KING Jr. London – GB † 1798
1008		KINGISSEP – SU
1009		LESZNO – PL
1010		ÖREBRO – S
1011		SZPROTAWA – PL
1012		ARBOGA – S

1013.		PRENZLAU – DDR
1014		ZNOJMO – CS
1015		FRANKFURT a. M. – D
1016		ANGERMÜNDE – DDR
1017		NÖRDLINGEN – D
1018		GDAŃSK – PL
1019		FRANKFURT a. M. – D
1020		REUTLINGEN – D
1021		AARAU – CH
1022		POSEN – PREUSSEN *Landmark*

1023		WRIEZEN – DDR
1024		Johann David RIEDER Aalen – D * 1674 † 1752
1025		ZEHDENICK – DDR
1026		GDAŃSK – PL
1027		MORAVSKÁ TŘEBOVÁ – CS
1028		KALININGRAD – SU
1029		Georg Balthasar GÜNTZLER Nördlingen – D M 1756 † before 1765
1030		BESANÇON – F
1031		Abraham CROWLEY Penrith – GB c. 1720–1760
1032		VILLINGEN – D

1033		POTSDAM – DDR
1034		NEURUPPIN – DDR
1035		Johann Gottfried **KANNENGIESSER** Drezdenko – PL B 1773 † 1800
1036		GORZÓW WIELKOPOLSKI – PL
1037		NEUCHÂTEL – CH
1038		ISNY – D
1039		SALZWEDEL – DDR from 1700
1040		MARKTREDWITZ – D
1041		Antoine ALÈGRE Angers – F 1776
1042		Jean Laurent DULAC Le Puy-en-Velay – F 1762

1043		William LANSDOWN Bristol – GB c. 1740
1044		Thomas HODGKIN West-Country – GB c. 1750–1770
1045		Samuel PIERCE Greenfield, Massachusetts – USA 1792–1830
1046		Samuel PIERCE Greenfield, Massachusetts – USA 1807–1830
1047		Jonathan COTTON Jr. London – GB second third of 18th cent.
1048		Thomas D. BOARDMAN Hartford – USA 1805–1820
1049		Thomas BADGER Boston – USA 1787–1815
1050		GRONINGEN – NL 15th cent.
1051		JÁCHYMOV – CS
1052		KEMPTEN – D

1053		KREMS – A
1054		LÜBECK – D
1055		Louis ALÈGRE Angers – F 1808–1835
1056		John BENSON London – GB c. middle of 18th cent.
1057		Edward GREGORY Bristol – GB first half of 18th cent.
1058		Mark of the Tsar's Court (owner) Moscow – SU
1059		Mark of the Tsar's Court Moscow – SU
1060		William CALDER Providence – USA 1817–1856
1061		Jehiel JOHNSON Middletown, Connecticut and Fayetteville, North Carolina – USA 1815–1825

1062 Blakslee BARNS
Philadelphia – USA
1812–1817

1063 Samuel DANFORTH
Hartford – USA
1795–1816

1064 Thomas DANFORTH
Stepney, Connecticut and
Philadelphia,
Pennsylvania – USA
1777–1818

1065 Parks BOYD
Philadelphia – USA
1795–1819

1066 Samuel KILBOURN
Baltimore – USA
1814–1830

1067 Ebenezer CROSSMAN
Hudson, New York – USA
c. 1790–1800

1068 J. and D. HINSDALE
Middletown, Connecticut –
USA
c. 1815

1069 Master M C I
Moscow – SU
18th cent.

1070 VILLERS & WILKES
Birmingham – GB
beginning of 19th cent.

1071		Samuel E. HAMLIN Providence – USA 1801–1856
1072		Charles PLUMLY Philadelphia – USA 1822–1833
1073		Otis WILLIAMS Buffalo, New York – USA 1826–1831
1074		Josiah DANFORTH Middletown, Connecticut – USA 1828–1837
1075		George LIGHTNER Baltimore – USA 1806–1815
1076		William DANFORTH Middletown, Connecticut – USA 1892–1820
1077		William NOTT Middletown, Connectitut and Fayetteville, North Carolina – USA 1813–1825
1078		Ashbil GRISWOLD Meriden, Connecticut – USA 1807–1815
1079		Johann Leonhard WILLHÖFER Erlangen – D 1831–1868

1080		Albrecht LIEDEL Hersbruck – D after 1822
1081		Robert KINNIBURGH Edinburgh – GB turn of 18th–19th cent.
1082		William HUNTER Edinburgh – GB third quarter of 18th cent.
1083		MOSCOW – SU
1084		KAPUSTIN Moscow – SU c. middle of 18th cent.
1085		TREPETOV Moscow – SU c. 1765
1086		David Osipov PEREKISLOV Moscow – SU court master from 1737
1087		Iov VASIĽEV Moscow – SU c. 1725

1088		Ustin PETROV Moscow – SU c. 1732
1089		Matheus SPOCK Gliwice – PL † 1808
1090		ŚCINAWA – PL
1091		CHEB – CS
1092		TESSIN – CH
1093		WERTHEIM – D
1094		MALMÖ – S
1095		SZCZECIN – PL
1096		HALE & SONS Bristol – GB third quarter of 19th cent.

1097		Luke JOHNSON London – GB first half of 18th cent.
1098		Johnson CHAMBERLAIN London – GB 18th cent.
1099		KAMENZ – DDR
1100		VILLACH – A
1101		VELKÉ MEZIŘÍČÍ – CS

PLANTS

1102		EKENÄS – SF
1103		EKSJÖ – S
1104		Michel van der LINDEN Tallinn – SU B 1777 † 1742
1105		Johann Leonhart PFEFFER Leipzig – DDR M 1738 † 1781

1106		Jürgen Dieterich HOLSTEIN Neubrandenburg – DDR M 1732 † 1764
1107		Carl Friedrich SEYBOLD Dresden – DDR M 1795
1108		Georg Paul UNOLD Sen. Kempten – D * 1777 † 1854
1109		Christian Gottlieb GOEBEL Dresden – DDR M 1765 † before 1785
1110		Gustav Adolf Eduard JAHN Dresden – DDR M 1835
1111		GADEBUSCH – DDR
1112		Gottfried GÖTZ Gdańsk – PL M 1725
1113		Gottfried Samuel TETZLAFF Elbląg – PL M 1843 (?) † 1866
1114		Hans Jacob LINDE Kiel – D M 1753 † 1792
1115		Johann Christian BÖHME Jr. Freiberg – DDR M 1755 † 1772

1116		Nicolaus ESSING Hamburg / Altona – D B 1729–1746
1117		Johann BUCHHOLTZ Flensburg – D M 1742
1118		Jürgen Jacob BORCHERT Grabow – DDR M 1758 † 1786
1119		Christian Bernhard BOECKENHAGEN Ribnitz – DDR M 1781 † 1823
1120		Johann Georg KRAUS Feuchtwangen – D second half of 18 cent.
1121		WAŁBRZYCH – PL
1122		Thomas ARNOTT London – GB beginning of 18th cent.
1123		Jacob GRÜNEWALD Stralsund – DDR B 1676 † 1728
1124		Johann Paul BÖHMER Dresden – DDR M 1752 † after 1785
1125		Francis WHITTLE London – GB first half of 18th cent.

1126		DIPPOLDISWALDE – DDR
1127		QUEDLINBURG – DDR
1128		Andreas GRÜNEWALD Jr. Greifswald – DDR M 1722
1129		Jochim WOHLERS Bergedorf – D M 1752 † 1791
1130		Peter GRÜNEWALD Stralsund – DDR B 1717–1732
1131		NOSSEN – DDR
1132		John WOODESON Chipping Wicomb, Bucks. – GB first quarter of 18th cent.
1133		Thomas J. T. ASHLEY London – GB second quarter of 19th cent. † 1852
1134		Jacob Heinrich SCHUMACHER Schwerin – DDR M 1721 † 1777
1135		Peter REESE Tallinn – SU B 1708 † 1754

1136		Gerth BLUHM Tallinn – SU B 1688 † 1705
1137		Theodore JENNINGS London – GB first half of 18th cent.
1138		Christoph FORCHHEIM Wrocław – PL M 1644 † 1667
1139		Johann Hinrich WULLF Eutin – D second third of 18th cent.
1140		Bernhard Christian BÖTTGER Lübeck – D M 1764 † 1811
1141		Caspar Christian GIERK Parchim – DDR M 1804 † after 1842
1142		Jürgen SIEBEN Jr. Lübeck – D B 1750 † 1793
1143		Johann Christian PLAGEMANN Lübeck – D B 1743 † 1766
1144		Robert MATTHEW London – GB first quarter of 18th cent.
1145		Samuel PRIDDLE London – GB second half of 18th cent.

1146		John PAXTON London – GB first quarter of 18th cent.
1147		Diedrich Christian AUGUSTINS Lübeck – D B 1764 † 1812
1148		Stephen COX Bristol – GB † 1754
1149		Samuel BOSS London – GB turn of 17th–18th cent.
1150		Henry BRASTED London – GB end of 17th cent.
1151		John BASKERVILLE London – GB end of 17th cent.
1152		William DREW Glasgow – GB c. 1800
1153		William CHARLESLEY London – GB † 1770
1154		William Cornelius SWIFT London – GB first third of 19th cent. † 1832
1155		RAPPERSWIL – CH

1156	William NEWHAM London – GB first quarter of 18th cent.
1157	Mathias RUNDQUIST Karlskrona – S 1778–1820
1158	Petter LAGERWALL Jönköping – S M 1739 † 1747
1159	EICHSTÄTT – D
1160	Melchior LEFFLER Visby – S 1748–1791
1161	Isaak LEHMANN Wittstock – DDR M 1648 † 1684
1162	Claus BONNEWITZ Lübeck – D B 1760 † 1777
1163	August Wenzel Ferdinand SCHÜTZ Wismar – DDR M 1843
1164	Johann Matthias TIMMERMANN Sen. Hamburg – D M 1744
1165	Johann Ludwig KUNST Hamburg / Harburg a. Elbe – D — M 1755–1779

1166		Gottfried KÖNIGSHAFEN Jr. Gdańsk – PL M 1731
1167		Johann KLEINFELDT Elbląg – PL M 1690
1168		Johann Friedrich PALISCH Sen. Bautzen – DDR M 1761
1169		Abraham Gottlieb KOHL Bautzen – DDR M 1685 † 1719
1170		Johann Tobias ECKERT Celle – D M 1728 † 1756
1171		Joachim Heinrich KAMPFFER Sen. Zagań – PL M 1696 † 1743
1172		Johann Heinrich SCHARP Sen. Hamm – D 1740 † 1768
1173		Georg BRANDL Karlovy Vary – CS c. 1750
1174		Henry APPLETON London – GB second half of 18th cent.
1175		CRAILSHEIM – D

1176	Johann Georg HALLBRITTER Crailsheim – D M 1794
1177	Hans ASMUSSEN Flensburg – D M 1723
1178	Johann Jacob KOOKE Eutin – D M 1760 † 1804
1179	Frantz Hinrich AHRENS Bergedorf – D 1731
1180	Jacob Hinrich OTTO Lübeck – D M 1750 † 1784
1181	Immanuel Gotthelf LUTTERE Dinkelsbühl – D * 1771 † 1842
1182	William FARMER London – GB c. middle of 18th cent.
1183	Johann Hermann MEYER Hamburg – D M 1802 † after 1830
1184	Edward LOCKWOOD London – GB † 1819
1185	Mark CRIPPS London – GB † 1776

1186		John BLENMAN London – GB first half of 18th cent.
1187		HANOVER – D
1188		LINDAU – D
1189		NAMYSŁOW – PL
1190		Hans Gottlieb BINTZ Bytom – PL first quarter of 18th cent.
1191		I. G. LOEFFLER Fürth – D M 1831
1192		Johann Georg JUNG Isny – D M 1747 (?) † 1777
1193		Johann Friedrich APPEL Celle – D M 1790 † 1826
1194		Christian APPEL Celle – D B 1758 † 1800
1195		John ANSELL London – GB first quarter of 18th cent.

1196		AUGSBURG – D
1197		AUGSBURG – D
1198		Friedrich KANDT Brzeg – PL * 1615 † 1669
1199		George Adam WERNER Strzelce Krajénskie – PL M 1741
1200		WEINFELDEN – CH
1201		Christoph RUPRECHT Augsburg – D M 1718
1202		NYSA – PL
1203		DEMMIN – DDR
1204		Johan ANJOU Gävle – S 1763–1804
1205		Simon REINBACHER Graz – A M 1803

1206		Michael HOLLÄNDER Schleswig – D M 1707 † before 1735
1207		Joachim BONNEWITZ Marne – D second half of 18th cent.
1208		François BEAUSSIER Angers – F 1732
1209		Gunder Pedersen SCHMIDT Odense – DK 1725
1210		ASH & HUTTON Bristol – GB c. 1760
1211		William WATKINS Bristol and Brecon – GB first half of 18th cent.
1212		HUMPHREY Exeter – GB c. 1730–1780
1213		John FERRIS & Co. Exeter – GB 1780–1795
1214		Henry HOSKYN Launceston – GB c. 1680–1730
1215		John FRENCH Bristol – GB last quarter of 18th cent.

1216		Robert BARNETT London – GB turn of 18th–19th cent. † 1829
1217		John BATCHELER Bristol – GB † 1713 (?)
1218		Master L F Paris – F 17th cent.
1219		N. F. MARCHAND Versailles – F 1737
1220		Louis Gabriel SAMAIN Montargis – F c. 1766
1221		Bernhard WICK Basel – CH M 1721 † 1747
1222		TRAUNSTEIN – D
1223		Johann Gottlieb LENTZ Kołobrzeg – PL B 1788
1224		Johann Friedrich Carl WINCLER Wismar – DDR M 1837 † 1845
1225		Robert RANDALL London – GB middle of 18th cent.

1226		Edward NASH London – GB first half of 18th cent.
1227		William HIGHMORE London – GB after 1741
1228		John JACKSON London – GB 1731–1743
1229		Robert MASSAM London – GB second third of 18th cent.
1230		George HOLMES London – GB after 1742
1231		STRASBOURG – F
1232		STRASBOURG – F
1233		SCHWYZ – CH
1234		Christoph DÜRR Annaberg – DDR M 1650 † 1682
1235		NEUMÜNSTER – D

1236		ELMSHORN – D
1237		FRIEDRICHSTADT – D
1238		FLENSBURG – D
1239		ECKERNFÖRDE – D
1240		TØNDER – DK
1241		HUSUM – D
1242		KIEL – D
1243		SCHLESWIG – D
1244		KAPPELN – D
1245		KIRCHHEIM unter Teck – D

1246		PENIG – DDR
1247		PYRZYCE – PL
1248		ROSENHEIM – D
1249		JINDŘICHŮV HRADEC – CS
1250		Gustav Wilhelm SCHAPKEWITZ Liepaja – SU 1764 † 1802
1251		Sven Bengtsson ROOS Göteborg – S 1768–1802
1252		Lorenz Joachim BEATOR Liepaja – SU M 1781
1253		Adrian GRETH Nysa – PL M before 1658 † 1700
1254		Johann Cristoph KORPISCH Świdnica – PL M 1699 † 1738
1255		Johann Peter LANIUS Bad Mergentheim – D turn of 18th–19th cent.

1256		Johann Frantz VOIGT Sen. Karlovy Vary – CS 18th cent.
1257		Justus Gottfried HOLSTEIN Osnabrück – D M 1767 † 1818
1258		Johann Christian Wilhelm BIERMANN Osnabrück – D M 1778–1817
1259		Eberhard Friedrich HOLSTEIN Osnabrück – D M 1808 † 1825
1260		John SMITH Edinburgh – GB c. 1730
1261		Sebald STOY Nuremberg – D first quarter of 17th cent.
1262		Robert BONYNGE Boston – GB 1731–1763 (?)
1263		Heinrich Christian STEINFORTH Zwischenahn-Bad – D M 1842
1264		Robert LOWELL Bristol – GB c. middle of 18th cent.
1265		F. van den BOGAARD 's Hertogenbosch – NL 19th cent.

1266		Johann JANSHEN Emden – D M 1829–1863
1267		Johann Reiners MÜLLER Leer – D * 1865–1929
1268		Johann Bernhard Christoph RONSTADT Leer – D * 1812–1860
1269		Philipp Herlyn van AMEREN Emden – D M 1842 † 1877
1270		Berend van MEKELENBORG Leer – D * 1751–1820 † 1834
1271		Diedrich BAHLMANN Quakenbrück – D * 1682 † 1745
1272		Johann MEINJOHANNS Papenburg – D 1867–1911
1273		Hilbert MÜHLENBERG Papenburg – D first quarter of 19th cent.
1274		Johann Gerberhard SCHULTE Quakenbrück – D * 1673 † 1741
1275		Theodor RONSTADT Leer – D * 1786 † 1837

1276		Wilhelm HATTERMANN I Aurich – D B 1700 † 1722
1277		Klaas ter WEE Aurich – D B 1849–1897
1278		Master I P NL end of 17th cent.
1279		Gerhard HULLMANN Cloppenburg – D * 1788 † 1860
1280		Anton HULLMANN Cloppenburg – D * 1753 † 1819
1281		Freerk van AMEREN Emden – D M 1814–1851
1282		Johann Christoph von der BURG Emden – D M 1743 † before 1792
1283		P. van DOORN Utrecht – NL
1284		Johann Friedrich Wilhelm BROCKMANN Hamburg – D M 1733 † before 1764
1285		Unknown master NL 17th cent.

1286		Johann George STIER Tallinn – SU B 1720 † 1767
1287		Jochim WEIß Tallinn – SU B 1657
1288		Johann Heinrich ECKHOLT Haselünne – D * 1744 † 1828
1289		Uve Willems Aden UVEN Norden – D * 1745 † 1833
1290		Gerhard Matthias HÖLSCHER Quakenbrück – D M 1787 † 1841
1291		Master I C R Brașov – R 18th cent. (?)
1292		John LANGTON London – GB second third of 18th cent.
1293		Carl GLAUCHE Miskolc – H 1835–1842
1294		Georg Friedrich BRAUN Györ – H M 1802–1825
1295		FOMA Moscow – SU 1725

1296		Anton ZAMPONI Wiener Neustadt – A 1818–1837 Mariazell – A 1837–1860s
1297		Johann Wilhelm STÜCKER Horní Slavkov – CS 18th cent.
1298		Frederick BASSETT New York – USA 1761–1780
1299		Leopold STADLER Budapest – H 1805–1836
1300		Anton HEILLINGÖTTER Karlovy Vary – CS M 1806
1301		Sebastian JURAME Budapest – H 1773–1791
1302		Johann WERWIZGI Györ – H M 1755–1788
1303		Peter MARCHIONINI Sopron – H 1803–1839
1304		Franz Ludwig ZIMM Vienna – A middle of 19th cent.

1305		John JUPE London – GB 1735 † 1781
1306		Archibald INGLIS Edinburgh – GB † c. 1777
1307		Joseph JEFFERYS London – GB third quarter of 18th cent.
1308		William BATHUS London – GB end of 18th cent.
1309		Henry SMITH London – GB first half of 18th cent.
1310		William BAMPTON London – GB 1742–1799 (?)
1311		John DOLBEARE Ashburton – GB † 1761
1312		Arthur WHARTON York – GB 18th cent.
1313		Joseph WINGOD London – GB 18th cent.
1314		Johann Anton SAGEMÜLLER Neuenburg – D M 1807 † 1839

1315		Hermann Wilhelm PETERSEN Tallinn – SU B 1767 † 1798
1316		James BUTCHER Jr. Bridgewater, Somerset – GB c. 1720
1317		Christoph Dietrich PETERSEN Varel – D 1750–1782
1318		Joseph LEDERER Györ – H 1773–1790
1319		Samuel Friedrich SCHULTZ Prague / Staré Město – CS M 1738 † 1771
1320		Josef Samuel MITTERBACHER Prague / Staré Město – CS M 1786 † 1805
1321		G. C. PITTEROFF Karlovy Vary – CS 18th cent.
1322		Abraham KUPFERSCHMIDT Tallinn – SU M 1758–1797
1323		MOSCOW – SU

1324		Ivan OSIPOV Moscow – SU c. 1742
1325		MOSCOW – SU

ARCHITECTURE

1326		NYKÖPING – S
1327		ZAGAŃ – PL
1328		John WEBBER Jr. Barnstaple – GB 1680–1735
1329		DÖMITZ – DDR
1330		DEGGENDORF – D
1331		KRONACH – D
1332		SIGHIŞOARA – R

1333		LICHTENSTEIN – DDR
1334		LAUENBURG a. Elbe – D
1335		HÄMEENLINNA – SF
1336		NYSLATT – SF
1337		BRUGG – CH
1338		BRUGG – CH
1339		LINZ – A
1340		WILSDRUFF – DDR
1341		OEDERAN – DDR
1342		J. P. PFEIFER Wiener Neustadt – A beginning of 18th cent.

1343		WIENER NEUSTADT – A
1344		FRANKENBERG – DDR
1345		MAGDEBURG – DDR
1346		SCHWEDT – DDR
1347		RADSTADT – A
1348		WAIDHOFEN a. d. Ybbs – A
1349		WELS – A
1350		ZIELONA GÓRA – PL
1351		PLAUEN – DDR
1352		PRAGUE / NOVÉ MĚSTO – CS

1353		WAREN – DDR
1354		ITZEHOE – D
1355		Johann Georg AUER Rothenburg a. d. Tauber – D M 1758
1356		HAVELBERG – DDR
1357		ČESKÁ LÍPA – CS
1358		STOLLBERG – DDR
1359		Alexander BROWN Edinburgh – GB first quarter of 18th cent.
1360		Andrew KINNEAR Edinburgh – GB second half of 18th cent.
1361		Alexander WRIGHT Edinburgh – GB 18th cent.
1362		John GLOVER Edinburgh – GB 18th cent.

1363		John LETHAM Edinburgh – GB † 1756
1364		William BALLANTYNE Edinburgh – GB 18th cent.
1365		JÖNKÖPING – S
1366		SOPRON – H 17th cent.
1367		SALZBURG – A
1368		FALKÖPING – S
1369		TRZEBIATÓW – PL
1370		Wilhelm Heinrich GUNDLACH Wismar – DDR M 1773–1814
1371		Peder HANSEN Copenhagen – DK 1656
1372		Hans HØY Copenhagen – DK M 1834

1373		SKARA – S
1374		LUND – S
1375		HÄLSINGBORG – S
1376		KALMAR – S
1377		WEILHEIM – D
1378		SPEYER – D
1379		BURGHAUSEN – D
1380		Friderich FRIDERICHSEN Copenhagen – DK M 1747
1381		BRATISLAVA – CS
1382		BAUTZEN – DDR

1383		BUDAPEST – H
1384		LÖSSNITZ – DDR
1385		DÖBELN – DDR
1386		DÖBELN – DDR c. 1700
1387		SOPRON – H
1388		MALBORK – PL
1389		BERGEDORF – D
1390		HAMBURG – D
1391		NEUBRANDENBURG – DDR
1392		HAMBURG – D

1393	GRIMMA – DDR
1394	ROCHLITZ – DDR
1395	ZĄBKOWICE ŚLĄSKIE – PL
1396	BYDGOSZCZ – PL
1397	CLUJ – R
1398	ZSCHOPAU – DDR
1399	HAMBURG / ALTONA – D
1400	BOLESŁAWIEC – PL
1401	CELLE – D
1402	LÜNEBURG – D

1403		FREIBERG – DDR
1404		PRAGUE / STARÉ MĚSTO – CS
1405		ČESKÉ BUDĚJOVICE – CS
1406		PRAGUE / MALÁ STRANA – CS
1407		STRZELCE KRAJÉNSKIE – PL
1408		FRIEDLAND – DDR
1409		RENDSBURG – D
1410		PLAU – DDR
1411		Matthaeus STARCK Neuötting – D B 1798
1412		Paul Philipp MESSIER Leutershausen – D M before 1732

1413		Jochim NEUENKIRCHEN Wismar – DDR M 1717 † 1754
1414		ÅMÅL – S
1415		Poul NIELSEN Aarhus – DK M 1751
1416		John SCHMIDT Køge – DK 1674
1417		Wenzeslaus LEONHARD Günzburg – D M 1795
1418		Eduard Ignatius NADLER Riga – SU 1836 † 1881
1419		Anton AICHER Sen. Altötting – D M 1803
1420		Nicolas RÖDER Budapest – H 1698–1712
1421		Thomas EDERT Budapest – H 1717–1741

1422		Joseph STAUDINGER Klagenfurt – A B 1813
1423		Daniel HITZ Chur – CH M 1817 (?)
1424		Canton GRAUBÜNDEN – CH
1425		Joseph SCHMIDT Most – CS first half of 19th cent.
1426		KARLSTAD – S
1427		Master I G E Litoměřice – CS 18th cent.
1428		MARBACH a. Neckar – D
1429		Johann Gottlieb ELIAS Legnica – PL M 1809–1828
1430		Gottlieb Benjamin SCHAMBERGER Legnica – PL * 1797 † 1823

1431		Ernst Hinrich Gotthelf ROESLER Zittau – DDR M 1825
1432		Ernst Wilhelm Gregor MÜLLER Löbau – DDR M 1825 † 1854

CELESTIAL BODIES AND SYMBOLS

1433		DUFLOS Le Mans – F 1748
1434		John ROGERS London – GB first half of 18th cent.
1435		John HOLLEY London – GB last quarter of 17th cent.
1436		John BELSON London – GB † 1783
1437		George BEESTON London – GB 18th cent.
1438		John HAYTON London – GB c. middle of 18th cent.
1439		GRANSON – CH
1440		John NEATON London – GB first half of 18th cent.

1441		Charles RANDALL London – GB c. 1700
1442		Thomas HUX London – GB first half of 18th cent.
1443		Hinrich Egidius JOBIN Annaberg – DDR third quarter of 18th cent.
1444		Görgen ROKUS Stockholm – S 1726–1759
1445		GRABOW – DDR
1446		G. VELLUT Amiens – F 1743
1447		RAKVERE – SU
1448		MERANO – I 16th cent.
1449		Christoph Ernst BORONSKY Elbląg – PL M 1686
1450		Carl Gotthold BREITFELD Annaberg – DDR M 1820 † 1869

1451	Master V C Aignay–le–Duc – F 1696
1452	PERLEBERG – DDR
1453	Johann Gottlob KRÜGER Wrocław – PL B 1820 † 1836
1454	DIESSENHOFEN – CH
1455	Mark of quality for *l'étain* *créé* F 1899
1456	Georg August HINRICHTS Varel – D * 1865 † 1950
1457	Hans PFRETZSCHNER Leipzig – DDR M 1645 † 1679
1458	KAUFBEUREN – D
1459	GOLENIÓW – PL
1460	Master W M ? Levoča – CS first half of 18th cent.

1461		Augustin GINTZEL Kłodzko – PL B 1791 † 1826
1462		Johann Jochim BRANDT Meldorf – D second third of 18th cent.
1463		J. MOUCEAU Aix-en-Provence – F 1696
1464		Johann Hinrich SCHLAPSY Sen. Hamburg – D B 1722 † 1749
1465		Johann Peter MARCKHARD Kiel – D M 1746 † 1773
1466		Ludolf Hinrich TROST Schleswig – D M 1778 (mark from 1781)
1467		Johann VOSS Jr. Rostock – DDR M 1745
1468		George WINTER London – GB first half of 18th cent.
1469		Thomas GIFFIN London – GB second half of 18th cent.
1470		Johann Christoph VOIGT Eberswalde – DDR M 1767 † 1790

1471		Caspar CONRADY Kappeln – D M 1756 † after 1780
1472		Ernst Julius Albert DRESSLER Dresden – DDR M 1837
1473		Hans Lorentz KUPFFERSCHMIDT Sen. Lübeck – D B 1726 † 1763
1474		Johann Hinrich PLAS I Hamburg – D M 1707 † 1749
1475		Joachim Andreas PAPE Celle – D M 1728 † 1753
1476		Andreas PAPE Celle – D M 1669 † 1707
1477		Johann PLAS II Hamburg – D M 1737 † 1771
1478		Johann Hinrich PLAS III Hamburg – D M 1770 † 1803
1479		Johan Heinrich PAPE I Celle – D * 1674 † 1724
1480		Wiedebald Rudolph GREVE Celle – D B 1716 † 1744

1481		Jürgen Friedrich **REINHARDT** Celle – D 1720 † 1743
1482		Martin **BRANDT** Hamburg – D M 1734 † before 1756
1483		LOVISA – SU

ITEMS

1484		Carl Adolph Ferdinand **HELDORN** Lübeck – D B 1854 † 1893
1485		Amand **WACKE** Ząbkowice Śląskie – PL end of 18th cent.
1486		Carl Gottl. **FISCHER** Jelenia Góra – PL M 1815
1487		Carl Gottlob **NOSTER** Oschatz – DDR M 1800 † 1841
1488		David **MELVILLE** Newport – USA 1776–1794
1489		Diedrich Hinrich **TIEDEMANN** Lübeck – D B 1835 (?) † 1850
1490		Master I W Haapsalu – SU 1770

1491	Master H S Narva – SU c. 1706
1492	Johann Gottlieb KLEIN Złotoryja – PL first quarter of 19th cent.
1493	William BILLINGS Providence – USA 1791–1806
1494	Olrik VÖSTHOFF Rostock – DDR M 1708–1723
1495	Friedrich Andreas HEROLD Hof a.d. Saale – D M 1808 (?)
1496	Daniel DEVEER Elbląg – PL M 1737
1497	Johann Christoph DÜRMER Leipzig – DDR M 1756–1785
1498	Ferdinand Thomas WECK Wrocław – PL B 1809–1835
1499	Johann Christoffer GEORGI Karlskrona – S 1731–1754
1500	Johann Jacob BIETAU Elbląg – PL M 1801 † 1842

1501		Jochim KRUMBÜGEL Güstrow – DDR M after 1730 † 1787
1502		Johann Peter LESCHHORN Rudna – PL M 1754 (?) † 1788
1503		Johann Wilhelm LEHMANN Kamenz – DDR M 1766 † 1779
1504		BRZEG – PL
1505		David MELVILLE Newport – USA 1776–1794
1506		Master I R Haapsalu – SU 1702
1507		TALLINN – SU
1508		EUTIN – D
1509		SCHWERIN – DDR
1510		KÖPING – S

1511		HERRNHUT – DDR
1512		Master I R Constance – D 18th cent. (?)
1513		Unkown master Bernay – F 18th cent. (?)
1514		Claude COUROYÉ Paris – F 1689
1515		Christopher WOOCK Anklam – DDR B 1721
1516		Johann Peter KUNST Anklam – DDR M 1707
1517		Thomas LEACH London – GB second third of 18th cent.
1518		Bernard BABB London – GB first half of 18th cent.
1519		William WIGHTMAN London – GB second half of 18th cent.
1520		Hans LAMBRECHT Wismar – DDR M 1703 † 1747

1521		ELBLĄG – PL
1522		LEVOČA – CS
1523		WSCHOWA – PL
•1524		Peter SCHUMACHER Demmin – DDR M 1767–1772
1525		I. LUSSEAU Tours – F 1759
1526		Johannes VETTERLE Landsberg a. Lech – D M 1765 (?) – 1790
1527		Johann SCHLICKER Hamburg – D M 1743
1528		Johann Hermann SCHLICKER Hamburg – D M 1777 † 1810
1529		Rudolf Hinrich HASSBERG Hamburg – D M 1731 † 1767
1530		KOŁOBRZEG – PL

1531		John HARTWELL London – GB second third of 18th cent.
1532		VAASA – SF
1533		FALUN – S
1534		STOCKHOLM – S
1535		UPPSALA – S
1536		Johann David KAYSER Szczecin – PL B 1751
1537		Johan Seben ONNECKEN Weener – D * 1826 † 1917
1538		HALMSTAD – S
1539		SIGTUNA – S
1540		LANDSKRONA – S

1541		James YATES Birmingham – GB c. 1800–1840
1542		Lukas MELDT Braşov – R 1701–1735
1543		Master M M Braşov – R 1761–1780
1544		W. HERMSEN Soest – D c. 1833 (?)
1545		Johann Baptista DEROSSI Bruchsal – D 1870 † 1912
1546		Christian Ludwig HOLTZ Westerhauderfehn – D after 1848
1547		Thomas SIMPKINS Boston – USA 1727–1766
1548		Joseph SPACKMAN & Co. London – GB c. 1785
1549		Ann TIDMARSH London – GB second quarter of 18th cent.
1550		SPACKMAN & GRANT London – GB first quarter of 18th cent.

1551		Lawrence LANGWORTHY Exeter – GB 1719
1552		John BASSET New York – USA 1720–1761
1553		Abraham WIGGIN London – GB first half of 18th cent.
1554		Martin EDMANN Bautzen – DDR M 1714 † 1745
1555		Joseph PITTROFF Karlovy Vary – CS 18th cent.
1556		Simon PATTINSON London – GB first half of 18th cent.
1557		MINDELHEIM – D
1558		Tobias SCHLEGEL Legnica – PL † 1672
1559		Hans WILD Jr. Jáchymov – CS M 1583
1560		Johann Joachim KLINGE Rehna – DDR M 1751 † 1781

1561		John WRIGHT London – GB 1717
1562		Johann Friedrich SIEFKEN Varel – D * 1841 † 1917
1563		CANNSTATT – D
1564		Caspar MEWES Sen. Parchim – DDR M 1670 † 1730
1565		Tobias KANNENGIESSER Prenzlau – DDR B 1695–1714
1566		Master I I P Györ – H c. 1728
1567		Andreas SCHRICK Sopron – H 1693–1730
1568		G. FRANK Sopron – H member of a family active 1740–1780
1569		Master G K Košice – CS 17th cent.
1570		Michael RICHTER Sopron – H 1718–1732

1571		Martin RICHTER Sopron – H 1732–1777
1572		Master M R Bratislava – CS c. 1744
1573		Georg Friedrich STOPR Prague / Staré Město – CS c. 1700
1574		Joh. Caspar DIEBL Prague / Nové Město – CS B 1706 † 1720
1575		Leonhard DÜRR Jáchymov – CS second half of 17th cent.
1576		Christoph BÖHMER Bratislava – CS Györ – H second half of 17th cent.
1577		Ernst KESTER Sopron – H 1668–1678
1578		Johann Christoph HÄRLEIN Künzelsau – D 1685 † 1729
1579		Master I R Bratislava – CS 19th cent.
1580		Andreas RODEMACHER Husum – D M 1811

1581		Friedrich Eckhard SPOHNHOLTZ Malchin – DDR M 1786 † 1811
1582		Caspar Matthias MÖLLER Wismar – DDR M 1740 † 1769
1583		A. TRABER Lucerne – CH second half of 17th cent.
1584		Andreas ROSS Oława – PL M 1675 (?) † 1718
1585		Richard HOLDEN Liverpool – GB c. 1760
1586		William SMITH London – GB 1732
1587		Joseph Philipp APELLER Innsbruck – A B 1754 † before 1809
1588		Reinhold Christoph H. TIETZE Świdnica – PL M 1820 † 1854
1589		Carl Gottlob KRAUSE Meissen – DDR M 1819–1852
1590		Martin RÖCKL Eichstätt – D first half of 19th cent.

1591	David CURTISS Albany – USA 1822–1840
1592	Jacob Friedrich VEIL Schorndorf – D M 1833 † 1850
1593	Joseph Henry GODFREY London – GB first quarter of 19th cent.
1594	Johann Gottlob RICHTER Celle – D B 1814 † 1830
1595	Adolf Gottlob Christian Wilhelm RICHTER Celle – D M 1838 † 1849
1596	HARTON & SONS London – GB 1680–1690
1597	Ludwig Wilhelm SCHRADER Celle – D M 1849 † 1886
1598	Master D S Sibiu – R c. 1746
1599	Master G B Sibiu – R 1712

1600		SIBIU – R
1601		STECKBORN – CH
1602		Jean Jacques PRÉVOST Paris – F 1732
1603		PIENIĘZNO – PL
1604		WITTSTOCK – DDR
1605		BÜTZOW – DDR
1606		BISCHOFSWERDA – DDR
1607		SOEST – D
1608		Canton NIDWALDEN – CH
1609		BREMEN – D

1610	STADE – D
1611	Georges GRAS Angers – F 1897–1925
1612	A. WEYGANG Öhringen – D contemporary mark of firm established in 1726
1613	Johann Abraham RAUSCHER Worms – D * 1705 † 1780
1614	Diederich BERTLING Wildeshausen – D * 1783 † 1821
1615	Friedrich Wilhelm NOLDE Wildeshausen – D * 1807 † 1864
1616	Johann Heinrich Wilhelm VOIGT Oldenburg – D B 1848 † 1891
1617	August WEYGANG Jr. Öhringen – D 1885 – takes over his father's workshop and uses the mark for utensils pro- duced according to older models
1618	Joseph Mauritz SCHMEDES Vechta – D * 1747 † 1801
1619	Johann Christian BAUMANN Delmenhorst – D 1761 † 1789

1620		Johann Christoph PAPE Oldenburg – D B 1830–1865 † 1882
1621		Johann Bernhard Anton ZELLER Delmenhorst – D * 1797 † 1842
1622		Nicolaus Gerhard HANSMANN Oldenburg – D M 1763 † 1808
1623		Bernhard Conrad FORTMANN Oldenburg – D * 1786 † 1833
1624		Paul Anton Detlev BAUMANN Oldenburg – D B 1786 † 1808
1625		PLZEŇ – CS
1626		NEUSTADT/GLEWE – DDR
1627		NEUCHÂTEL – CH
1628		POZNAŃ – PL
1629		LUBAŃ – PL

1630		LEGNICA – PL
1631		RIGA – SU
1632		POZNAŃ – PL
1633		BUXTEHUDE – D
1634		Master P C Bordeaux – F 18th cent.
1635		PÄRNU – SU
1636		TARTU – SU
1637		NAUMBURG a. d. Saale – DDR
1638		STRZEGOM – PL
1639		STRÄNGNÄS – S

1640		KULDIGA – SU
1641		TRNAVA – CS
1642		RUDNA – PL
1643		RATTENBERG – A
1644		ERFURT – DDR
1645		MÖLLN – D
1646		MÜHLDORF a. Inn – D
1647		Franz ABRELL Mühldorf a. Inn – D first quarter of 19th cent.
1648		Richard BOWCHER London – GB first half of 18th cent.
1649		John CARR London – GB c. 1700

1650	Frédéric DOLLFUS Mulhouse – F 1754–1768
1651	Jean Jacques BRUCKER Mulhouse – F 1738–1795
1652	Hans BIRR Mulhouse – F * 1631 † 1675
1653	Johann Maria Elias NOTARIS Iburg – D third quarter of 18th cent.
1654	Lübbert Diedrich BAHLMANN Quakenbrück – D * 1710 – third quarter of 18th cent.
1655	Christoph Diederich STEINMÖLLER Jr. Hamburg / Altona – D M 1766
1656	STRAUBING – D
1657	MAINZ – D
1658	SÖDERHAMM – S
1659	Benjamin FELSKE Gdańsk – PL M 1673

1660		HORN – A
1661		URACH – D
1662		HORNEBURG – D
1663		Friedrich Heinrich BIEMANN Hamburg – D M 1820 † after 1852
1664		James BULLOCK London – GB c. middle of 18th cent.
1665		Robert JACKSON London – GB end of 18th cent.
1666		Roger MOSER London – GB beginning of 19th cent.
1667		James FIDDES London – GB third quarter of 18th cent.
1668		Ralph BENTON London – GB end of 17th cent.
1669		William WALKER London – GB end of 18th cent.

1670		David BROCKS London – GB beginning of 18th cent.
1671		Thomas HAWKINS London – GB third quarter of 18th cent.
1672		Thomas COLLET London – GB second quarter of 18th cent.
1673		ZOFINGEN – CH
1674		Friedrich Wilhelm GRANZOW Sen. Dresden – DDR M 1818 † 1878
1675		FASSON & SONS London – GB c. 1784–1810
1676		Melchior SCHWARTZ Sen. Görlitz – DDR B 1651 † 1703
1677		LANDSHUT – D
1678		Daniel BARTON London – GB first quarter of 18th cent.
1679		Claude ANTÉAUME Paris – F M 1743

1680		Alois SALVER Ellwangen – D M 1791 † 1832
1681		Richard NEWMAN London – GB * 1747 † 1780
1682		Robert Piercy HODGE London – GB last quarter of 18th cent.
1683		Edward SIDEY London – GB c. 1773
1684		Johann Caspar WAGE Parchim – DDR M 1740 † 1765
1685		HERRNHUT – DDR
1686		Nathaniel MEAKIN Jr. London – GB (?) second half of 18th cent.
1687		Wilhelm August DENGELHAUSEN Wrocław – PL B 1726–1868
1688		Stephan SCHELLING Ulm – D M 1716 (?) – 1765
1689		Johann Anton MELLY Bamberg – D M 1730 † before 1776

1690		E. LAURÉOUX Paris – F 1896–1905
1691		BOPFINGEN – D
1692		HELSINKI – SF
1693		Andreas OESTMANN Sen. Szczecin – PL B 1756
1694		KRISTINEHAMM – S
1695		SCHANDAU – DDR
1696		VÄSTERVIK – S
1697		Archibald & William COATS Glasgow – GB c. 1800
1698		Stephen MAXWELL & Co. Glasgow – GB c. 1800
1699		GRAHAM & WARDROP Glasgow – GB c. 1776–1806

1700		Ebenezer SOUTHMAYD Castleton, Vermont – USA 1802–1820
1701		William ALDER Sunderland – GB c. 1700
1702		Catesby CHAPMAN London – GB first half of 18th cent.
1703		Thomas DODSON London – GB second half of 18th cent.
1704		Franz Ludwig WOLF Jr. Bischofswerda – DDR M 1846
1705		Johann Hinrich BOHT Eckernförde – D M 1719
1706		Nicolaus Ehring PETERSEN Eckernförde – D M 1736 † 1763
1707		Master C B S T Schwyz – CH end of 17th cent.
1708		I. ARMAND Besançon – F 1766
1709		François SERGENT Avallon – F 1730

1710		Edme Olivier de CESNE Triel – F M 1736 † before 1780
1711		Charles Augustin FEBVRE Arras – F 1727
1712		Pierre MALMOUCHE Le Mans – F 1747
1713		Jean PIRONNEAU Paris – F 1726
1714		Unknown master Abbeville – F beginning of 18th cent.
1715		René PARAIN Paris – F 1763
1716		André François BOICERVOISE Paris – F M 1741
1717		Jean TARDIF Paris – F 1716
1718		Simon LEFÈVRE Paris – F 1684
1719		Michel NAIL Calais – F 1745

1720		Jean TARDY Paris – F c. 1716
1721		Toussaint JOUFFROY Besançon – F 1676
1722		Jean-Baptiste BLANC Espalion – F 1770
1723		J. PETITOT Flavigny – F c. 1693
1724		Abraham KUPFERSCHMIDT Tallinn – SU B 1758–1797
1725		James LETHARD London – GB middle of 18th cent.
1726		Stephen Kent HAGGER London – GB third quarter of 18th cent.
1727		John LANGFORD London – GB 1780
1728		ESKILSTUNA – S
1729		Gotthardt Diederich KOCH Hamburg – D M 1768 † 1780

1730		BORÅS – S
1731		ALTENBERG – DDR
1732		TARNOWSKIE GÓRY – PL
1733		SALA – S
1734		ALTENBERG – DDR
1735		MARIENBERG – DDR
1736		SCHNEEBERG – DDR
1737		SCHWARZENBERG – DDR
1738		EIBENSTOCK – DDR
1739		JOHANNGEORGENSTADT – DDR

1740		ANNABERG – DDR
1741		BEČOV nad Teplou – CS
1742		BAIA-MARE – R
1743		MEISSEN – DDR mark for newer utensils resembling older ones
1744		BIEL – CH
1745		SCHORNDORF – D
1746		EIBENSTOCK – DDR
1747		Carl BEHMANN II Oldenburg – D 1934–1942
1748		GEISING – DDR
1749		Robert KNIGHT London – GB last quarter of 18th cent.

1750		Richard MISTER London – GB beginning of 19th cent. † 1839
1751		John WINGOT London – GB from middle of 18th cent. † 1784
1752		CARPENTER & HAMBERGER London – GB end of 18th cent.

TOUCHES

1753		OLDENBURG – D
1754		Master H S Cluj – R 17th cent.
1755		BANSKÁ BYSTRICA – CS
1756		KOŠICE – CS
1757		LOHR a. Main – D
1758		Bengt STÅHLSTRÖM II Kalmar – S 1742–1765
1759		BISTRIŢA – R

1760		HORB a. Neckar – D
1761		ZUG – CH
1762		FREYSTADT – A
1763		STARGARD SZCZECIŃSKI – PL
1764		ZOFINGEN – CH
1765		SOLOTHURN – CH
1766		ULM – D
1767		BOLZANO – I
1768		WALLIS – CH
1769		LUCERNE – CH

1770		BURGDORF – CH
1771		BEROMÜNSTER – CH
1772		VEVEY – CH
1773		GYÖR – H
1774		BREGENZ – A
1775		OPAVA – CS
1776		Frantz Caspar SCHMIDT Sen. Würzburg – D M 1733 † after 1766
1777		Lorentz STEGER Würzburg – D M 1728 † 1756
1778		Georg Stephan SEITZ Gerolzhofen – D M 1745 † after 1772
1779		COLMAR – F

1780		NANCY – F
1781		STRASBOURG – F
1782		STRASBOURG – F
1783		KARLSRUHE – D
1784		ANSBACH – D
1785		BADEN–BADEN – D
1786		RHEINECK – CH
1787		LEISNIG – DDR
1788		THUN – CH
1789		WALDENBURG – DDR

1790		Johann Michael **SCHAEFER I** Ansbach – D M 1750–1785
1791		**MARIESTAD – S**
1792		**RIED – A**
1793		**SCHÄRDING – A**
1794		**DINGOLFING – D**
1795		**JAWOR – PL**
1796		**BADEN – CH**
1797		**GEROLZHOFEN – D**
1798		**TŘEBÍČ – CS**
1799		**LEIPZIG – DDR**

1800		FELDKIRCH – A
1801		MONTFORT – CH
1802		TÜBINGEN – D
1803		Johann Daniel ALTENBERGER Kitzingen – D M 1733 † 1786
1804		STRALSUND – DDR
1805		ANKLAM – DDR
1806		BACKNANG – D
1807		DRESDEN – DDR
1808		MEISSEN – DDR
1809		Gustav Friedrich GÜNTZLER Uffenheim – D M 1793

1810		PENZLIN – DDR
1811		WISMAR – DDR
1812		BRIG – CH
1813		Hans Jacob LOCKER III Memmingen – D 1740 † 1756
1814		RACIBÓRZ – PL
1815		SALZWEDEL – DDR
1816		BYTOM – PL
1817		LWÓWEK ŚLĄSKI – PL
1818		STENDAL – DDR
1819		GARDELEGEN – DDR

1820		PREŠOV – CS
1821		OPOLE – PL
1822		Nicolaus HORCHAIMER Nuremberg – D M 1561 † 1583
1823		Michel RÖSSLER Sen. Nuremberg – D M 1596 † 1635
1824		Hans Sigismund GEISSER Nuremberg – D M 1652 † 1682
1825		Albrecht PREISSENSIN Nuremberg – D M 1564 † 1598
1826		Andreas DAMBACH Nuremberg – D M 1627 † 1650
1827		Andreas MERGENTHALER Nuremberg – D M 1596 † 1635
1828		Paulus ÖHAM Jr. Nuremberg – D M 1634 † 1671
1829		Caspar WADEL Jr. Nuremberg – D M 1656 † 1706

1830		Hans SPATZ I Nuremberg – D from end of 16th cent. † 1641
1831		Jacob KOCH III Nuremberg – D 1609 † 1630
1832		Lorentz APPEL Nuremberg – D M 1630 † 1658
1833		Melchior HORCHAIMER Nuremberg – D M 1583 † 1623
1834		Hans SPATZ II Nuremberg – D M 1630 † 1670
1835		Zacharias SPATZ Nuremberg – D M 1661 † 1713
1836		Johann Gottfried HILPERT Nuremberg – D M 1760 † 1801
1837		Johann Gottfried ROTHE Nuremberg – D M 1767 † 1804
1838		RIBEAUVILLÉ – F
1839		PASEWALK – DDR

1840		CREUSSEN – D
1841		BALINGEN – D
1842		MÜNCHBERG – D
1843		FREIBURG (Brsg.) – D
1844		BAD MERGENTHEIM – D
1845		KULMBACH – D
1846		ROTTERDAM – NL
1847		WUNSIEDEL – D
1848		Joseph DITTL Vienna – A M 1750 † after 1787
1849		Lorenz DENGLER Vienna – A B 1719

1850		Franz SCHIMMER Vienna – A B 1761
1851		Hans Caspar VOGL Vienna – A B 1705
1852		Hans Jacob SANDIG Vienna – A B 1679
1853		Johann Elias WEYGANDT Vienna – A B 1684
1854		Johann Georg SIBERN Vienna – A B 1729
1855		Johann Joseph HICKMANN Vienna – A B 1731 † before 1763
1856		Gottfried ZELS Vienna – A M 1756
1857		GLAUCHAU – DDR
1858		WALDENBURG – DDR
1859		BÉTHUNE – F

1860		Johann Christian BAYER Györ – H 1737–1748
1861		Master G L D Kaufbeuren – D middle of 18th cent.
1862		Johann Nepomuk VOGLER Constance – D M 1783
1863		Carl Wilhelm SEIFFERT Mannheim – D M 1807 † c. 1840
1864		Johann Leonhard HAERTLE Cham – D M 1844 † 1912
1865		Benjamin BACON London – GB second half of 18th cent.
1866		HAMM – D
1867		Carl HASELBACH Legnica – PL * 1803 (?) † 1875
1868		William de JERSEY London – GB † 1785

1869		William PHIPPS London – GB c. middle of 18th cent.
1870		Richard BAGSHAW London – GB last quarter of 18th – beginning of 19th cent.
1871		William ROWELL London – GB first half of 18th cent.
1872		Jonathan LEACH London – GB 18th cent.
1873		Robert GALBRAITH Glasgow – GB c. 1840
1874		Robert STANTON London – GB † 1842
1875		BURFORD & GREEN London – GB 18th cent.
1876		William Glover ANNISON London – GB c. middle of 18th cent.
1877		Thomas BOARDMAN London – GB † 1773

COMBINED TOUCHES

1878		Johannes GMÜNDER St. Gallen – CH * 1630 † 1678

1879		Isaak DINNER Glarus – CH * 1683 † 1734
1880		David ZWEIFEL Glarus – CH * 1767 * 1818
1881		Franz CLOSTERMAYR Ingolstadt – D M 1679
1882		Johannes FÖSSL Graz – A M 1720
1883		Bartholomeus AMMAN Ermatingen – CH M 1778
1884		Andreas WÜGER IV Steckborn – CH M 1777
1885		BRAUNAU a. Inn – A
1886		Johann Conrad SCHALCH III Schaffhausen – CH * 1764 † 1826
1887		Master H I E Sargans – CH end of 18th cent.
1888		Gottfried ALDE Kamienna Góra – PL † 1781

1889		Joseph Anton LECHNER Salzburg – A M 1756 † 1771
1890		Sigmund HITZINGER Neuburg a. Donau – D † 1734
1891		Georg Ferdinand WEILHAMMER Salzburg – A B 1720 † 1749
1892		Franz HÖFLER Mattighofen – A M 1756
1893		Rochus KESTELBERGER Gmunden – A M 1696 1709 leaves for Linz
1894		Joseph REDÁCZY Sopron – H 1782–1803
1895		Adam Friedrich WIEDAMANN Regensburg – D 1821 † 1860
1896		Emerich GÜNTZER Regensburg – D M 1673 † after 1892
1897		Johann Baptist BRIDLER Bischofszell – CH * 1751 † 1805
1898		Joachim Leonz KEISER Zug – CH * 1728 † 1809

1899		W. Jacob RIETER Winterthur – CH 1750–1796
1900		Hans PETER Elgg – CH turn of 18th–19th cent.
1901		Salomon WIRZ Zürich – CH M 1766 † 1815
1902		G. CANIS Jr. Appenzell – CH first half of 19th cent.
1903		Joseph LEDERER Györ – H M 1773–1790
1904		Unkown master Györ – H 18th–19th cent.
1905		Johann Gottlob ZIMMERMANN Debrecen – H after 1822
1906		Christian Philipp LEUTWEIN Schwäbisch Hall – D third quarter of 18th cent. † after 1871
1907		Ignatz GANSEL Plzeň – CS 1790–1813

1908		Christoph EHERMANN Brno – CS B 1675
1909		Franz PFUNDT Brno – CS B 1699
1910		Paul LANG Brno – CS B 1739 † 1778
1911		Christoph SCHRAMEL Brno – CS M 1750
1912		Carl Josef HUCK Olomouc – CS M 1743
1913		Marek Antonín JEDLIČKA Olomouc – CS M 1751–1771
1914		Joseph GRUBER Olomouc – CS M 1751–1765
1915		Johann Georg HAAN Olomouc – CS M 1768
1916		Franz HANTSCH Jihlava – CS B 1737
1917		Johann Adam AICHMAYR Linz – A M 1716 † 1746

1918		Rochus KESTELBERGER Linz – A B 1709 † 1714
1919		Joseph Anton GREISSING Salzburg – A B 1698 † 1740
1920		Andreas PÖCK Linz – A M 1725 † 1749
1921		Johann Franz RÖDERER Linz – A M 1707 † c. 1750
1922		Johann Caspar RÖTTER Innsbruck – A M 1742–1809
1923		Andreas Johann DIEBL Prague / Malá Strana – CS M 1687 † 1747
1924		Anton PAMBERGER Linz – A M 1656–1692
1925		Johann Ludwig PAMBERGER Linz – A M 1683 † 1708
1926		Josef Samuel MITTERBACHER Prague / Staré Město – CS M 1786 † 1805

1927		Johann Jacob STRETTI Celje – YU M 1793
1928		Joseph Bernhard MEINING Straubing – D M 1756 † before 1774
1929		Hans Felix SOMMERAUER Zürich – CH † 1714
1930		Johannes HARDER Constance – D M 1718–1762
1931		Johann Peter RITTNER Altdorf – D M 1806
1932		Hermann Joseph BOSCH (?) Mainz – D middle of 18th cent.
1933		Anton David STROBACH Braniewo – PL B 1776 † 1793/94
1934		Christoph LIPMANN Elbląg – PL M 1771 † 1788
1935		Christoph WOLFF Elbląg – PL M 1712 † 1736

1936		Daniel TOCK Elbląg – PL M 1721 † 1750
1937		Johann Daniel DEVEER Elbląg – PL M 1762 † 1798
1938		David KROLL Malbork – PL M 1776
1939		Simon NEUBAUER Braniewo – PL B 1743
1940		Eva PETERSEN (pewterer's widow) Riga – SU head of workshop from 1724 † 1766
1941		Abraham HAYEN II Riga – SU M 1780 † 1798
1942		Johan HAYEN I Riga – SU B 1707 † 1752
1943		Johann Gottlieb GREIFF Kaliningrad – SU M 1767
1944		Johann Wilhelm FELDTMAN Jelgava – SU M 1795–1826

1945		August Anton **PREUSCHOFF** Braniewo – PL M 1826 † 1852
1946		Johann Gottfried RANCK Kaliningrad – SU M 1756
1947		Peter PELET Jr. Kaliningrad – SU B 1792

ORIENTAL TOUCHES

1948	南錫	Mark of quality for products made of an alloy of 95 per cent tin (Sn) J from 1890
1949	錫	Mark of quality for products of an alloy of 99 per cent tin (Sn) J from 1890
1950	錫嘉	Suzu-ka J after 1940
1951	錫本	Suzu-han J c. 1910
1952	號乾造茂	Mark of quality for pewter products with an alloy of 80 per cent tin (Sn) J since 1890 (original master's touch of an outstanding pewterer)

| 1953 | | Hsing-shun
Ch'ao-yang, Swatow – RC
19th cent. |

1953

Hsing-shun
Ch'ao-yang, Swatow – RC
19th cent.

1954

Yen-hsing-shun
Ch'ao-yang, Swatow – RC
19th cent.

1955

Liang-i
RC
19th cent.

1956

Yamasaki
Taniyama, Kagoshima
Prefecture – J
19th cent.

1957

Yen-hsing-shun
Ch'ao-yang, Swatow – RC
19th cent.

1958

I-ho-shun
RC
19th cent.

1959

Yüan-shun
RC
19th cent.

1960

Yen-pien-ho
Shan-ti, Swatow – RC
19th cent.

INDEX OF PLACES

Colmar – F, 1779
Cologne – D, 322
Constance – D, 1512, 1862, 1930
Copenhagen – DK, 589, 1371, 1372, 1380
Corcaigh see Cork – IRL
Cork (Corcaigh) – IRL, 314, 716, 717, 999
Coventry – GB, 843
Crailsheim – D, 1175, 1176
Creussen – D, 1840

Danzig see Gdańsk – PL
Debrecen – H, 1905
Děčín (Tetschen) – CS, 707
Deggendorf – D, 1330
Delmenhorst – D, 1619, 1621
Demmin – DDR, 208, 1203, 1524
Detern – D, 16, 271
Diessenhofen – CH, 1454
Dijon – F, 981
Dingolfing – D, 1794
Dinkelsbühl – D, 1181
Dippoldiswalde – DDR, 1126
Döbeln – DDR, 710, 786, 1385, 1386
Dömitz – DDR, 1329
Dorpat see Tartu – SU
Dortmund – D, 557, 572, 593
Dresden – DDR, 484, 941, 974, 1107, 1109, 1110, 1124, 1472, 1674, 1807
Drezdenko (Driezen) – PL, 1035
Driezen see Drezdenko – PL
Dublin (Baile átha Cliath) – IRL, 280, 281, 291–293, 299, 321, 607, 955, 1005
Dzierżoniów (Reichenbach) – PL, 447, 474, 800

Eberswalde – DDR, 395, 877, 1470
Eckernförde – D, 70, 1239, 1705, 1706
Edinburgh – GB, 298, 304, 305, 391, 1081, 1082, 1260, 1306, 1359–1364
Eger see Cheb – CS
Eggenfelden – D, 724, 980
Eglisau – CH, 798
Eibenstock – DDR, 491, 1738, 1746

Eichstätt – D, 1159, 1590
Ekenäs – SF, 1102
Eksjö – S, 144, 1103
Elbing see Elbląg – PL
Elbląg (Elbing) – PL, 40, 41, 845, 1113, 1167, 1449, 1496, 1500, 1521, 1934–1937
Elgg – CH, 1900
Ellwangen – D, 1680
Elmshorn – D, 582, 1236
Emden – D, 1266, 1269, 1281, 1282
English Bicknor, Glos. – GB, 686
Enns – A, 722
Eperies see Prešov – CS
Eperjes see Prešov – CS
Erfurt – DDR, 1644
Erlangen – D, 1079
Ermatingen – CH, 864, 1883
Esens – D, 587, 592
Eskilstuna – S, 1728
Espalion – F, 1722
Essen – D, 128
Esslingen – D, 43, 105
Eutin – D, 1139, 1178, 1508
Evreux – F, 836
Exeter – GB, 317, 858, 1212, 1213, 1551

Falköping – S, 1368
Falun – S, 781, 1533
Fayetteville – USA, 1061, 1077
Feldkirch – A, 1800
Feuchtwangen – D, 1120
Flavigny – F, 1723
Flensburg – D, 62, 471, 1117, 1177, 1238
Frankenberg – DDR, 1344
Frankenstein see Ząbkowice Śląskie – PL
Frankfurt a. Main – D, 47, 48, 495, 500, 538, 576, 1015, 1019
Frankfurt a.d. Oder – DDR, 985
Frauenfeld – CH, 453
Fraustadt see Wschowa – PL
Freiberg – DDR, 626, 651, 1115, 1403
Freiburg (Brsg.) – D, 455, 1843
Freising – D, 777
Freystadt – A, 1762
Freystadt see Kozuchów – PL

235

Friedeberg see Strzelce Krajén-
skie – PL
Friedland – DDR, 807, 1408
Friedrichstadt – D, 1237
Friesoythe – D, 83
Fürstenau – D, 49
Fürth – D, 1191

Gadebusch – DDR, 920, 942,
1111
Gardelegen – DDR, 1819
Gävle – S, 52, 54, 1204
Gdańsk (Danzig) – PL, 31, 230,
241, 253, 1018, 1026, 1112,
1166, 1659
Geising – DDR, 1748
Gerolzhofen – D, 1778, 1797
Giengen – D, 762
Glarus – CH, 1879, 1880
Glasgow – GB, 267, 1152, 1697-
1699, 1873
Glatz see Kłodzko – PL
Glauchau – DDR, 410, 1857
Gleiwitz see Gliwice – PL
Gliwice (Gleiwitz) – PL, 1089
Glogau see Głogów – PL
Głogów (Glogau) – PL, 55, 439
Gloucester – GB, 685
Glückstadt – D, 194, 227, 487
Gmunden – A, 1893
Gnoien – DDR, 102, 921
Goldberg see Złotoryja – PL
Goldingen see Kuldiga – SU
Goleniów – PL, 1459
Göppingen – D, 930, 931
Görlitz – DDR, 652, 653, 1676
Gorzów Wielkopolski – PL,
485, 507, 1036
Göteborg – S, 60, 693, 1251
Grabow – DDR, 76, 233, 1118,
1445
Granson – CH, 1439
Graubünden (Canton) – CH,
1424
Graz – A, 80, 116, 642, 643,
1205, 1882
Greenfield – USA, 1045, 1046
Greifenberg see Gryfów Śląski –
PL
Greifswald – DDR, 29, 107, 236,
741, 878, 1128
Grimma – DDR, 830, 1393

Grobinya – SU, 550
Groningen – NL, 1050
Grossenhain – DDR, 735, 803
Groß-Meseritsch see Velké Me-
ziříčí – CS
Grünberg see Zielona Góra – PL
Gryfów Śląski (Greifenberg) –
PL, 50, 452, 740
Günzburg – D, 1417
Güstrow – DDR, 36, 37, 114, 224,
464–466, 774, 775, 811, 1501
Györ (Raab) – H, 273, 296, 517,
1294, 1302, 1318, 1566, 1576,
1773, 1860, 1903, 1904

Haapsalu – SU, 1490, 1506
Hainichen – DDR, 269
Halmstad – S, 1538
Hälsingborg – S, 79, 1375
Hamburg – D, 46, 71, 193, 199,
228, 229, 232, 249, 275, 315,
417, 475, 516, 559, 562, 565,
570, 571, 747, 748, 1164, 1183,
1284, 1390, 1392, 1464, 1474,
1477, 1478, 1482, 1527–1529,
1663, 1729
Hamburg/Altona – D, 198, 220,
254, 255, 489, 548, 556, 563,
564, 567, 953, 1116, 1399, 1655
Hamburg/Harburg – D, 641, 950,
1165
Hämeenlinna – SF, 1335
Hamm – D, 1172, 1866
Hanover – D, 1187
Harburg a. Elbe see Hamburg/
Harburg – D
Härnösand – S, 849
Hartford – USA, 1048, 1063
Haselünne – D, 61, 543, 1288
Havelberg – DDR, 469, 1356
Hedemora – S, 74, 152
Heide – D, 32, 88, 396, 443, 472
Heidenheim – D, 386
Heilbronn – D, 89
Helsinki – SF, 1692
Hermannstadt see Sibiu – R
Herrnhut – DDR, 1511, 1685
Hersbruck – D, 1080
Hertogenbosch see 's Hertogen-
bosch – NL
Hirschberg see Jelenia Góra –
PL

Tallinn (Reval) – SU, 2, 3, 7, 35, 66, 67, 94, 109, 131, 189, 204, 207, 209–211, 237–239, 246, 288, 415, 488, 502, 511–513, 515, 580, 616, 771, 783, 1104, 1135, 1136, 1286, 1287, 1315, 1322, 1507, 1724

Taniyama, Kagoshima Prefecture – J, 1956

Tarnowskie Góry – PL, 1732

Tartu (Yur'ev, Dorpat) – SU, 13, 103, 176, 258, 259, 287, 503, 514, 1636

Teplice (Teplitz) – CS, 382

Tessin – CH, 1092

Teterow – DDR, 899

Tetschen see Děčín – CS

Thun – CH, 1788

Tiverton – GB, 835

Tölz – D, 727

Tønder – DK, 470, 1240

Tours – F, 1525

Traunstein – D, 750, 1222

Třebíč – CS, 1798

Treptow see Trzebiatów – PL

Triel – F, 1710

Trnava – CS, 1641

Troppau see Opava – CS

Truro – GB, 673

Trzebiatów (Treptow) – PL, 1369

Tübingen – D, 934, 1802

Turku (Åbo) – SF, 1, 106

Uddevalla – S, 175

Uelzen – D, 871

Uffenheim – D, 1809

Ulm – D, 448, 1688, 1766

Uppsala – S, 699, 713, 1535

Urach – D, 453, 1661

Uri – CH, 895

Utrecht – NL, 1283

Uusikaupunki – SF, 143

Vaasa – SF, 1532

Vänersborg – S, 146, 182

Varberg – S, 120, 183, 873

Varel – D, 551, 1317, 1456, 1562

Västerås – S, 136, 617

Västervik – S, 821, 1696

Vaxjö – S, 23

Vechta – D, 1618

Velké Meziříčí (Groß Meseritsch) – CS, 1101

Venice – I, 757

Versailles – F, 1219

Vesoul – F, 725

Vevey – CH, 1772

Vienna – A, 1304, 1848 – 1856

Villach – A, 1100

Villingen – D, 1032

Vilshofen – D, 731

Vimmerby – S, 65, 184

Visby – S, 178, 1160

Vyborg – SU, 181

Waidhofen a.d.Ybbs – A, 1348

Wałbrzych (Waldenburg) – PL, 1121

Waldenburg – DDR, 1789, 1858

Waldenburg see Wałbrzych – PL

Wallis – CH, 1768

Waren – DDR, 91, 1353

Wasserburg a. Inn – D, 640, 658

Waterford – IRL, 424, 907

Waxjö – S, 180

Weener – D, 1537

Weiden – D, 536

Weilheim – D, 1377

Weinfelden – CH, 1200

Wels – A, 847, 1349

Wertheim – D, 1093

Wesenberg see Rakvere – SU

West-Country – GB, 1044

Westerhauderfehn – D, 1546

Westerstede – D, 553

Wiener Neustadt – A, 1296, 1342, 1343

Wigan – GB, 290, 768, 951

Wil – CH, 866

Wildeshausen – D, 1614, 1615

Wilsdruff – DDR, 1340

Winnenden – D, 933

Winterthur – CH, 733, 1899

Wismar – DDR, 5, 222, 1163, 1224, 1370, 1413, 1520, 1582, 1811

Wittenberg – DDR, 926

Wittstock – DDR, 501, 1161, 1604

Wolgast – DDR, 745

Worms – D, 1613

INDEX OF NAMES

Basedow, Johann Jacob, 115
Baskerville, John, 1151
Bass, Johann Jochim, 91
Basset, John, 1552
Bassett, Frederick, 45, 1298
Batcheler, John, 1217
Bathus, William, 1308
Batteson, Thomas, 976
Baumann, Gottlob Friedrich, 69
Baumann, Johann Christian, 1619
Baumann, Paul Anton Detlev, 1624
Bayer, Johann Christian, 1860
Beamont, William, 718
Beathon, Anton Christian, 432
Beator, Lorenz Joachim, 1252
Beaussier, François, 1208
Becherer, Andreas Christoph, 940
Bechlin, F., 775
Beckendorff, Christian Jacob, 194
Becker, Joh., 316
Beeston, George, 1437
Behmann I, Carl, 16
Behmann II, Carl, 1747
Beindorf, Christian Ludwig, 495, 538
Belson, John, 1436
Bennet, Thomas, 686
Bennet, Thomas, 728
Benham, J., 276
Benson, John, 1056
Benton, Ralph, 1668
Berg, Lars, 126
Berger, Christoph, 483
Berglund, Sven, 171
Bergman, Magnus, 137
Berner, Johann Georg, 931
Bertling, Diederich, 1614
Bertzow, Jochim Christoph David, 192
Bessant, Nathaniel, 917
Beyer, Johann Joseph, 697
B I, 550
Biedermann, Jeremias, 406
Biemann, Friedrich Heinrich, 1663
Biermann, Johann Christian Wilhelm, 1258

Bietau, Johann Jacob, 1500
Billing, Samuel, 843
Billings, William, 1493
Binner, Mattheus, 749
Bintz, Hans Gottlieb, 1190
Birch &Villers, 915
Birr, Hans, 1652
Bishop, James, 390
Björkman, Eric, 825
Blanc, Jean-Baptiste, 1722
Blasius, Johann Gottlieb, 938
Blenman, John, 1186
Bluhm, Gerth, 1136
Boardman, Thomas, 1877
Boardman, Thomas D., 1048
Bodecker, Johan Henrik, 831
Boeckenhagen, Christian Bernhard, 1119
Boeckmann, Gottlob Friedrich, 934
Bogaard, F. van den, 1265
Böhm, Sigismund Gottlieb, 705
Böhme Jr., Johann Christian, 1115
Böhmer, Carl Adolph, 459
Böhmer, Christoph, 1576
Böhmer, Johann Paul, 1214
Bohnekamp, Jacob Conrad, 590
Boht, Johann Hinrich, 1705
Boicervoise, André François, 1716
Boicervoise, Nicolas, 147
Boldt, Hans Wilhelm, 409
Bonkin, Jonathan, 402
Bonnewitz, Claus, 1162
Bonnewitz, Joachim, 1207
Bonynge, Robert, 1262
Borchers, A. Carl Clemens, 5
Borchert, Jürgen Jacob, 1118
Borchwardt, Daniel Friedrich, 37
Borocco Sen., Peter Joseph, 155
Boronsky, Christoph Ernst, 1449
Borst, Jacques Frédéric, 506
Bosch (?), Hermann Joseph, 1932
Boss, Samuel, 1149
Boteführ, Christian Joachim Friedrich, 195
Boteler, John, 714

Cripps, Mark, 1185
Crooke, Robert, 822
Crossman, Ebenezer, 1067
Crowley, Abraham, 1031
C S, 488
Curtis & Co., 449
Curtis, James, 450
Curtiss, David, 1591

Dackombe, Aquila, 893
Dadley see Pitt & Dadley
Dahlin, Andreas, 191
Dahm, Johann Friedrich Thomas, 315
Dahm, Johann Hinrich, 199
Dambach, Andreas, 1826
Dambach, Franz, 377
Damm, Carl Moritz, 979
Danforth, John, 681
Danforth, Joseph, 683
Danforth, Josiah, 1074
Danforth, Samuel, 1063
Danforth, Thomas, 663, 1064
Danforth, Thomas II, 682
Danforth, William, 1076
Davis, John, 583
Dengelhausen, Wilhelm August, 1687
Dengler, Lorenz, 1849
Derossi, Johann Baptista, 1545
Deveer, Daniel, 1496
Deveer, Johann Daniel, 1937
Diebl, Andreas Johann, 1923
Diebl, Joh. Caspar, 1574
Dinner, Isaak, 1879
Dittl, Joseph, 1848
Dodson, Thomas, 1703
Doerffel, Johann Andreas, 827
Dolbeare, John, 1311
Dolfus, Philippe, 555
Dollfus, Frédéric, 1650
Donne, Joseph, 623
Doorn, P. van, 1283
Dörflig, Carl August Wilhelm, 974
D P R, 494
Dreptin, Catherine, 283
Dreptin, E., 678
Dresco, L., 127
Dressler, Ernst Julius Albert, 1472
Drew, William, 1152

D R K, 39
Drühl, Georg Christian Gottfried, 71
Drühl, Joachim Christian, 99
Drühl, Johann Friedrich Christian, 213
Drühl, Johann Gottlieb, 214
D S, 1598
Duflos, 1433
Dulac, André, 670
Dulac, Jean Laurent, 1042
Duncomb, Samuel, 918
Dürmer, Johann Christoph, 1497
Dürr, Christoph, 1234
Dürr, Leonhard, 1575

Eberhard, Carl Christoph, 386
Ebert, Benjamin Gottlob, 948
Ebert I, Paul Friedrich, 804
Ecke Sen., Caspar, 815
Eckelmann, Andreas Ludwig, 190
Eckelmann, Johann Balthasar, 97
Eckert, Johann Tobias, 1170
Eckholt, Gerhard Heinrich, 61
Eckholt, Heinrich, 75
Eckholt, Johann Gerhard, 543
Eckholt, Johann Heinrich, 1288
Edert, Thomas, 1421
Edgar & Son, P., 451
Edmann, Martin, 1554
Edwards, John, 796
Ehermann, Christoph, 1908
Ekström, Sven, 168
Elias, Johann George, 454
Elias, Johann Gottlieb, 1429
Elliot, Bartholomew, 420
Ellis, Samuel, 842
Elsworth, William J., 839
Emmerich, Johann Michael, 612
Englefield, William James, 857
Epler, Peter Jacob, 255
Essing, Nicolaus, 1116
Everett, James, 628
Everett, James, 630
Ewen, John, 620
Excell, James, 384
Eylers, Johan Anton, 268

Fagerström, Johan Petter, 119
Fahrenkrüger, Bernhard Johann, 193

Gräpcke, Christian Hinrich, 747
Gräpcke, Hans Christian, 748
Gras, Georges, 1611
Grave, Goerg Lambert Matthias, 571
Graves, Jean, 982
Gray & King, 944
Green see Burford & Green
Green, John Gray, 458
Green, Samuel, 300
Green, William Sandys, 751
Greenfell, George, 753
Greffet, Rollin, 674
Gregory, Edward, 1057
Greiff, Johann Gottlieb, 1943
Greissing, Joseph Anton, 1919
Grell, Christian, 208
Greth, Adrian, 1253
Greve, Wiedebald Rudolph, 1480
Griffin see Townsend & Griffin
Griffith, John, 754
Grimes & Son, 261
Griswold, Ashbil, 1078
Grossmann, Johann Gottfried, 492
Groth, Hans Christian Thomas, 88
Groth, Otto Friedrich, 438
Gruber, Joseph, 1914
Grünewald Jr., Andreas, 1128
Grünewald, Jacob, 1123
Grünewald, Johann Conrad, 541
Grünewald Sen., Peter, 878
Grünewald, Peter, 1130
Gulielminetti, Bernhard, 698
Gundlach, Wilhelm Heinrich, 1370
Günther, Friedrich Albert, see Liedemann, Johan Ferdinand & Günther, Friedrich Albert
Güntzer, Emerich, 1896
Güntzler, Georg Balthasar, 1029
Güntzler, Gustav Friedrich, 1809
Gurnell, John, 779

Haan, Johann Georg, 1915
Haas, Andreas, 880
Hacker, Diedrich, 35
Haertle, Johann Leonhard, 1864
Hagelstein, Heinrich Cornelius Martin, 570

Hagger, Stephen Kent, 1726
Hahn, Rosina, 493
Halbritter, Johann Georg, 1176
Hale & Sons, 1096
Halford, Simon, 756
Hamberger see Carpenter & Hamberger
Hamilton, Alexander, 376
Hamlin, Samuel, 289
Hamlin, Samuel E., 1071
Hamphie, Alexander, 1005
Handy, William, 627
Hansen, Peder, 1371
Hansmann, Claus, 231
Hansmann, Nicolaus Gerhard, 221, 1622
Hantsch, Franz, 1916
Harder, Johannes, 1930
Härlein, Johann Christoph, 1578
Harms, Lüdecke, 251
Harris, William, 912
Harrison, John, 687
Harsch, Johann Joseph, 116
Harton see Watts & Harton
Harton & Sons, 1596
Hartwell, John, 1531
Harvey, Edmund, 983
Haselbach, Carl, 1867
Haselbach, Johann Gottfried, 73
Hassberg, Rudolf Hinrich, 1529
Hattermann I, Wilhelm, 1276
Hausherr, Christian Volrath, 30
Hausherr, Detloff Andreas, 36
Hawkins, Thomas, 1671
Hayen II, Abraham, 1941
Hayen I, Johan, 92, 1942
Hayen III, Johann, 574
Hayter, George, 375
Hayton, John, 1438
Heaney, John, 607
Hecht, Jochim, 889
Hedecken, Georg Wilhelm, 70
Hediger, Max, 584
Hegewaldt Jr., Johann George, 805
Heillingötter, Anton, 1300
Heillingötter, Joseph, 411
Heising, Peter Heinrich, 573
Heitmann, Joachim Christopher, 101

Löwe, Peter Hinrich, 668
Lowell, Robert, 1264
L T, 131
Lüders, Johann, 565
Lukaffsky, Adam Heinrich, 566
Lukianov, Andrei, 349, 372
Lundén, Pehr Henrik, 159
Lusseau, I., 1525
Luttere, Immanuel Gotthelf, 1181
Lutz, Joseph, 547

Maas, Georg Christoph, 946
Mackenzie, William, 301
Madame, Friedrich Ferdinand, 455
Mägebehr, Johann, 234
Maier, Philipp Friedrich, 405
Makeev, Vasilei, 360
Makiov, Vasilei, 361
Malmouche, Pierre, 272, 1712
Mansrieder, Jacob, 846
Manz, Hans Rudolf, 499
Marchand, N. F., 1219
Marchionini, Peter, 1303
Marckhardt, Johann Peter, 1465
Martin, Pierre, 609
Martini, Gottfried, 528
Massam, Robert, 1229
Matthew, Robert, 1144
Matthiessen, Friedrich, 46
Matton, Kaspar, 837
Maxey, Charles Puckle, 1001
Maxwell & Co., Stephen, 1698
M C I, 1069
Meakin Jr., Nathaniel, 1686
Meckseper, Johann Christian, 559
Meese, Johann Adolph, 254
Meese, Peter, 247
Meining, Joseph Bernhard, 1928
Meinjohanns, Johann, 1272
Mekelenborg, Berend van, 1270
Meldt, Lukas, 1542
Melly, Johann Anton, 1689
Melville, David, 1488, 1505
Merckel, Hans Wilhelm, 85
Mergenthaler, Andreas, 1827
Merry, Martin, 321
Mescheder, Anton, 800
Messier, Paul Philipp, 1412
Metzel, Johann Siegfried, 501

Meunier, Martin, 984
Mewes Sen., Caspar, 1564
Meyer, Andreas Heinrich, 418
Meyer, Gottlieb Wilhelm August, 206
Meyer, Hermann Daniel, 614
Meyer, Johann Hermann, 1183
Meyer, Jacob Hinrich, 198
Meyer, Jürgen III, 250
Meyer, R., 544
Michel, Andries, 797
Mikhailov, Ivan, 347, 371
Miller, Johann Christoph, 763
Mister, Richard, 1750
Mitchell see Wood & Mitchell
Mitterbacher, Josef Samuel, 1320, 1926
Mix, Johann Friedrich, 133
M K, 141
M M, 486
M M, 1543
Moberg, Martin Gustaf, 142
Möller, Caspar Matthias, 1582
Monk, Joseph, 752
Moody, John Boucher, 312
Morane, P., 151
Morant, Laurent, 388
Morse, Robert, 715
Moser, Roger, 1666
Moskov, 329
Moskovskoi, 339
Mouceau, J., 1463
M R, 1572
Mühlenberg, Hilbert, 1273
Muhlert, J. P., 366
Müller, Balthasar Wilhelm, 439
Müller, Ernst Wilhelm Gregor, 1432
Müller, Georg Heinrich, 792
Müller, Johann Peter Wilhelm, 793
Müller, Johann Reiners, 1267
Munday, Thomas, 393
Munster Iron Co., 717
Müssiggang, Johann Gottlieb, 961

Nadler, Eduard Ignatius, 1418
Nail, Michel, 1719
Nash, Edward, 1226
Neaton, John, 1440

Neeff, Johann Georg, 500
Neidhardt, Joseph, 522
Nettlefold, William, 958
Neubauer, Simon, 1939
Neuenkirchen, Jochim, 1413
Neumann, Carl Gottlieb, 484
Neumann, Daniel, 242
Neumann, Johann Christoffer, 414
Newham, William, 1156
Newman, Richard, 1681
Nicolai, Friedrich Wilhelm, 185
Nielsen, Poul, 1415
Nieröse, Melchior Friedrich, 485
Nikiforov, Nikolai, 350
Nolde, Friedrich Wilhelm, 1615
Norén, Petter Samuelsson, 152
Norfolk, Richard, 719
Noster, Carl Gottlob, 1487
Notaris, Johann Maria Elias, 1653
Nott, William, 1077
Nussmann, Anton, 446

Oechslin, Johann Alexander, 924
Oesterling, Carl Christoph Friedrich, 32
Oestmann Sen., Andreas, 1693
Öham Jr., Paulus, 1828
Öhlerg, Petter, 158
Ohrdorf, Johan Heinrich, 963
Olding, Johann Heinrich, 112
Onnecken, Johann Seben, 1537
Orion, 324
Orivit, 322
Ormiston, John, 955
Osborne, John, 692
Osipov, Antip, 363
Osipov, David, 336
Osipov, Ivan, 334
Osipov, Ivan, 1324
Osipov, Yakov, 335
Osiris, 323
Otterer, Michael, 257
Otto, Jacob Hinrich, 1180
Ötzmann, Georg, 434

Page, Thomas, 759
Palheydt, Johann, 225
Palisch Jr., Johann Friedrich, 1168

Pamberger, Anton, 1924
Pamberger, Johann Ludwig, 1925
Pape, Andreas, 1476
Pape, Joachim Andreas, 1475
Pape, Johan Heinrich I, 1479
Pape, Johann Christoph, 1620
Parain, René, 1715
Parham, Benjamin, 986
Parker, Thomas, 689
Parr, Norton, 999
Patience, Robert, 601
Pattinson, Simon, 1556
Paxton, John, 1146
P C, 1634
Pedder, Joseph, 989
Pelet, Friedrich, 523
Pelet Jr., Peter, 1947
Pelletier, Louis, 132
Perekislov, David Osipov, 1086
Peter, Hans, 1900
Peters, Friedrich Christian, 551
Petersen, Christoph Dietrich, 1317
Petersen, Eva, 1940
Petersen, Hermann Wilhelm, 288, 513, 1315
Petersen, Nicolaus Ehring, 1706
Petitot, J., 1723
Petrov, Ustin, 337, 1088
Pewes, Benjamin, 230
Pfeffer, Johann Leonhart, 1105
Pfeifer, J. P., 1342
Pfister, Hans Bernhardt, 80
Pfretzschner, Hans, 1457
Pfundt, Franz, 1909
Phillips, Thomas, 634
Phipps, William, 1869
Pierce, Samuel, 1045, 1046
Pilz, Traugott Friedrich August, 626
Pironneau, Jean, 1713
Pissavy, Pierre, 307
Pitt & Dadley, 854
Pitteroff, G. C., 1321
Pittroff, Joseph, 1555
Plagemann, Johann Christian, 1143
Plagemann, Johann Wilhelm, 548
Plas, Johann Hinrich I, 1474
Plas, Johann II, 1477